Libraries

You may return this book to any Camden library
For a full list please see www.camden.gov.uk

For terms and conditions of library membership
www.camden.gov.uk/libraries

For 24 hour renewals
www.camden.gov.uk/libraries and click renew
(library card and pin number needed)

Tel: 020 7974 4444 for all library enquiries

Under Balkan Light

Selected Writings 5: Part 3, The Balkan Trilogy

RICHARD BERENGARTEN was born in London in 1943, into a family of musicians. He has lived in Italy, Greece, the USA and former Yugoslavia. His perspectives as a poet combine English, French, Mediterranean, Jewish, Slavic, American and Oriental influences.

Under the name RICHARD BURNS, he has published more than 25 books. In the 1970s, he founded and ran the international Cambridge Poetry Festival. He has received the Eric Gregory Award, the Wingate-Jewish Quarterly Award for Poetry, the Keats Poetry Prize, the Yeats Club Prize, the international Morava Charter Poetry Prize and the Great Lesson Award (Serbia). He has been Writer-in-Residence at the international Eliot-Dante Colloquium in Florence, Arts Council Writer-in-Residence at the Victoria Centre in Gravesend, Royal Literary Fund Fellow at Newnham College, Cambridge, and a Royal Literary Fund Project Fellow. He has been Visiting Associate Professor at the University of Notre Dame and British Council Lecturer in Belgrade, first at the Centre for Foreign Languages and then at the Philological Faculty. He is currently a Bye-Fellow at Downing College, Cambridge and Preceptor at Corpus Christi College, Cambridge. His poems have been translated into 22 languages.

By Richard Berengarten

Under Balkan Light

SELECTED WRITINGS
Volume 5
The Balkan Trilogy : Part 3

RICHARD BERENGARTEN

CAMBRIDGE

PUBLISHED BY SALT PUBLISHING
14a High Street, Fulbourn, Cambridge CB21 5DH United Kingdom

© Richard Berengarten, 2008

The right of Richard Berengarten to be identified as the
author of this work has been asserted by him in accordance
with Section 77 of the Copyright, Designs and Patents Act 1988.

First published 2008

Printed and bound in the United Kingdom by Biddles Ltd, King's Lynn, Norfolk

Typeset in Swift 9.5 / 13

ISBN 978 1 84471 439 1 hardback

Salt Publishing Ltd gratefully acknowledges
the financial assistance of Arts Council England

1 3 5 7 9 8 6 4 2

In memory of Ivan V. Lalić

Contents

Editorial Note

Under Balkan Light is the fifth volume published in 2008 in the on-going Salt series of Richard Berengarten's *Selected Writings*. It is also the last part of his *Balkan Trilogy*, following *The Blue Butterfly* and *In a Time of Drought*. For more than twenty-five years, the author has maintained a close involvement with the life, culture and politics of the Balkans. Between 1987 and 1991, he spent three years living and working in Yugoslavia. This stay coincided with the years in which the Yugoslav Federation was beginning to break apart in a series of violent conflicts. The author lived in Croatia and Serbia, and travelled in Macedonia, Slovenia, Montenegro, Bosnia and Hercegovina, Vojvodina and Kosovo. Since then he has repeatedly returned to Serbia and Slovenia.

Under Balkan Light collects the varied poems that Richard Berengarten has written out of this knot of experiences over a twenty-one year period between September 1987 and August 2008.

Acknowledgements

Thanks to the editors who have previously published the following poems: 'Do vidjenja Danitse', *Sibila*, Brazil, http://sibila.com.br/Home.html, 2008. 'Ned Goy has gone out' and 'Bogomil', *The London Magazine*, April/May 2002 and December/January 2003. 'A wallet' and 'Fish soup', *Mencard*, Menard Press, 2003, and *Stride Magazine*, 2006. 'White Cherries', *Stride Magazine*, 2006. 'On the Qualities of Light in the Balkans, *The Wolf*, London, 2005. 'Poem at the Autumn Equinox', *Against Perfection*, The King of Hearts, Norwich, 1999, and *The Mind Has Mountains*, Los Poetry Press, Cambridge, 1999. 'Poem for my infant daughter at Mileševa Monastery' and 'What do you mean by it', *Serbian Literary Magazine*, Serbian Writers' Association, Belgrade, 2006/1. 'Guests', *Against Perfection*, The King of Hearts, Norwich, 1999. 'Fragment, on The Sepharad', *SaLon*, No. 9, London, 1998. 'In War, June 1943', *The Jewish Quarterly*, London, No. 148, Winter 1992–3. 'Poem for a very small child', *Chanticleer Magazine*, No. 4, Edinburgh, 2003. 'Father to Small Child', *Los Poetry Press*, Cambridge, poemcard, December 2001. 'Borderers', *Wasafiri*, No. 53, London, February 2009. 'The Voice in the Garden', *For the Living*, first edition, Salt Publishing, Cambridge, 2004. 'Even when you lived', 'Nobody dies too late' and 'Lords of the far side', *Notre Dame Review*, No. 26, Indiana, Summer, 2008. 'On the Death of Ivan V. Lalić, *Almanac*, Ulaanbaatar, Mongolia, 2008.

The cover reproduces part of the fresco of the Angel at Christ's Tomb in Mileševa Monastery in southwest Serbia. The source for the photographs on pp. 19–26 and 44–45 is *The Crimes of the Fascist Occupants and their Collaborators Against Jews in Yugoslavia* (Federation of Jewish Communities of the Federative People's Republic of Yugoslavia, Belgrade, 1957), pp. 225–245. The drawing of the Neretva

Bridge at Mostar on p. 145 comes from Arthur Evans's *Through Bosnia and the Herzegovina on Foot During the Insurrection, August and September, 1873, with an Historical Review of Bosnia and a Glimpse of the Croats, Slavonians and the Ancient Republic of Ragusa* (Longmans, Green & Co, London, 1876, p. 344).

My special thanks go to my partner, Melanie Rein, for her constant support while I was putting this book together in the summer of 2007. For their valuable comments and suggestions during the final editing of this book, I should also like to thank Sonja Besford, Danica Čanković, Paul Scott Derrick, Philip Kuhn, Jasna Levinger-Goy, Andrija Matić, Vera V. Radojević and Anthony Rudolf. Finally, for their tireless patience and support in bringing this book out, my thanks to Chris and Jen Hamilton-Emery at Salt Publishing.

RB
CAMBRIDGE
SEPTEMBER 3, 2008

1   Do vidjenja Danitsé

Goodbye Balkan Belle

Uvek si mi draga bila
(Always you have been dear to me)

Yugoslav Song

And I will give him the morning star

Revelations 2 : 28

Danitsé with your bitter black cherries and heavenly
lilac abundant on hillsides and your nightingales
VOŽDOVAC   pouring song all spring long
          over sprawling city gardens
through throats purged of every mortal impurity
as if by the translucent flame of *rakija*, insidiously
ZLATIBOR   steeping unsuspecting hillsides
          in a longing for immortality;
Danitsé with your autumns outdoing their damnedest
to imitate the gaudy gone sunsets of summertime
by layering and crumbling all conceivable hues
MRČAJEVCI   of fire on your fields,
          villages, rocks, trees;
Danitsé of willows and lindens, Danitsé of owls and swallows,
Danitsé of oaks and birches, Danitsé of maze-making bees
moaning, adrift and roving among flowers and corpses
as if they could annul time with cool liquid gold; Danitsé
among punch-drunk butterflies mating in the rubble
SMEDEREVO   of fortresses where ghosts
          of solitary sentinels
tonight as forever will patrol their starry vigil, over
moonbathed ramparts floodlit by rippling waters
for distant Caesars, Pashas, Sultans, Czars, Führers,
none of whom gives a damn for you now, nor ever did;
Danitsé treading precarious foam-washed rocky promontories
ZADAR, TROGIR   bordering a blue more intense
          than cobalt glass, whose gulls wheel
over white-stoned palaces tucked into curling bays and
harbours decked out like watery gardens, blossoming
OMIŠ, ŠIBENIK   in sails and buzzing with
          ferries and fishing boats
about to chug away to chattering clucking islands
BRAČ, HVAR   where mimosa blazes in
          January and swallows
nest in eaves and swirl on summer air, as if reluctant

[3]

RAGUSA   to abandon them, ever,
for Africa; Danitsé of living
merchant cities and jumbled neglected peripheries whose

SALONAE   remains of amphitheatres, clogged
with ivy and bindweed,
overlook straits once lorded by pirates,
edge-dwellers, bandits, borderers, outsiders,

SENJ   corsairs, pounders, pouncers,
Uskoks, Vlachs, Morlachs,
where toppled pillars, overgrown with nettles,
point towards rocky roads, that curl away up slopes

KAŠTEL STARI   for lambs and goats to graze
on perfumed grass among
vines and water melons, then teeter into mountains
among whose rocks, in seams and fissures, cling
villages peopled by shepherds, farmers, butchers,

SINJ   footballers, basketball champions,
climbers, jousters, believers
in pagan faith healings; my complex, wayward,
joyeuse-triste jolie-laide contradictory Danitsé,

SARAJEVO   with far too many cross-winds
ruffling your hair for your own
peace, comfort or security; moody Danitsé, wearing
a thousand faces and expressions inside a minute;
my tolerant spontaneous opinionated unpredictable
Danitsé soaked in perfumes, rouge-caked, dancing,
laughing fluently behind lip-paint and mascara; Danitsé
in the park where children scream their prowess
on tricycles to gaggles of adoring aunts and grannies

KALEMEGDAN   while grandads play chess,
surrounded by gangs
of neighbours, all commentating, analysing, cussing,
all experts, all specialists, all Kasparovs, all Karpovs,
as if again they were braggart-boys in playgrounds long

[4]

BEŽANIJA disappeared under tower blocks;
nose-held-high Danitsé, walking
your thoroughbred, pestered by insistent mongrels
UŠČE   at the confluence of rivers;
nobody's and everybody's dangerous
come-and-get-me-if-you-dare Danitsé sipping cocktails
in the Star Bar in the new Hotel International and
Hotel Global and Hotel Startime and Hotel Galactic
where mobster bosses hung out, and one, biggest
and ugliest of the big-time thugs, got gunned down
with a henchman, and they never caught who did it;
Danitsé, not knowing who did it, but knowing for sure
nobody-till-time-end will ever admit to knowing; Danitsé
SMEDEREVO   spooning fish soup followed by forkfuls
of fried squid, while a solo gypsy fiddler,
in a provincial restaurant, floor sprinkled with sawdust,
plays *Silken Thread* for workers on Friday evenings
PETROVARADIN   and *Stop Flowing River*
and *It Ain't Worth Crying*
and *My Sweet Little Marijana* and *I've Just One Wish*
SKADARLIJA   and *My Man Milan* and *Days*
When I Don't Know What I'll Do;
gone seventeen year old Danitsé surveying the ravine
from the prow of the world's most elegant river-bridge
MOSTAR   where daredevil boys once dive-
bombed thirty metres into
currents below; petite student Danitsé, exuding
gigantesque exuberance and vitality, sauntering
homewards through alleyways at three-thirty a.m.
NOVI PAZAR   stopping by a back door,
wide open, near the mosque,
familiar since childhood, to chat to the moustachioed
baker stoking his furnace, who once sat grinning
in the row behind you in junior school, carving
initials into his desktop, pulling your pigtails,

pinching you as far below your waist as he
could safely reach, without teacher noticing,
whispering your first swearwords; Danitsé-age-seven.
pony-tailed, curly, beribboned, playing with imported
Barbies, satchel on back, striving for five out of five
for *Nature and Society* and *Artistic Culture*; Danitsé

SKOPJE running errands to the market
lined with coffee houses, scented
with Turkish delight, chocolate, toffee, nougat;
Danitsé buying corn-dolls, pistachio nuts, peanuts,

BAŠČARŠIJA sunflower seeds, almonds
and unchewable jelly babies
in coils of coarse grey paper; Danitsé shelling chestnuts
toasted on autumnal braziers, savouring the crisp

VODNIK and soft white bits, spitting
out the charred, into gutter
wayside, flowerbed; Danitsé at the fairground,

ZOOLOŠKI VRT first on the little Big Wheel,
then on the dodgems;
Danitsé at the hairdresser; Danitsé spending two days,
morning till evening, preparing dishes for your Saint's
Day, setting out the feast on lace-bordered tablecloths,

PALILULA with matching serviettes and
doilies tatted by Grandmother,
lined in old tissue paper, sliding them out of
their leather case with hardened corner pads;
Danitsé, queenly, welcoming, accepting stiff

DEDINJE bouquets of nostril-blocking
waxen creamy yellow lilies;
Danitsé washing and cleaning, after the party's end,
emptying wine-flooded ashtrays, wiping down, polishing,
ironing, starching, relining your whole trousseau in

VOJVODE STEPE fresh tissue paper; Danitsé
descending from seventh
floor, ferrying knotted trash-filled plastic bags

[6]

to be chucked into wheely bins where the poor
rummage for stale bread, newspapers, cardboard;
Danitsé trudging cobbles; Danitsé screeching your
midget car to a halt at traffic lights where crippled

SREMSKA   gypsy children hawk newspapers
packed with handfuls of wan roses
and plead for the privilege of cleaning your dusty
windscreen; Danitsé speeding past listing trucks
with one light or no lights; Danitsé cursed and

NUŠIĆEVA   cursing, when everything grinds
to a halt, as it does frequently; dare-
devil Danitsé, honking and gesticulating, overtaking

KNEZA MILOŠA   on the inside, ready to fight
your passage through everything
and take on all-comers for your individual space

AUTOKOMANDA   to edge forward
on the unrepaired pitted
motorway – southwards past Monument Hill

AVALA   towards fields and forest –
that might get resurfaced
one day; Danitsé home in your ancestral village,

ŠUMADIJA, BANAT, VOJVODINA   collecting eggs
among barnyard-
roaming hens; Danitsé churning sour cream to
textures of precise perfection, preparing soft
cheese, yoghurt, paper thin pastry, spinach-

ZELENI VENAC, BAJLONOVA   filled pies to drive
to market tomorrow
where you'll hover all day behind a trestle table

KALENIĆ, DUŠANOVA   along with other
countrywomen wearing
white smocks and overalls, each preoccupied

ZEMUN, DJERAM   with milk, each offering
forkfuls to tempt purchasing
housewives; Danitsé caught unawares, overcome

[7]

by peacefulness, first pealing and tumbling, then
stealing your spirit away, calling you into sleep
followed by a wakefulness steeped in the perfume
MILEŠEVA, DEČANI   of privet scented gardens
                tucked among hills, protected
by impoverished monasteries with peeling stucco walls,
crumbling arched colonnades, and cool interiors blessed
SOPOĆANI, MORAČA   by tall gazes of saints,
                presiding glances of angels,
undamaged lords and ladies of distant imagined heavens
watching down the centuries: eyes unbearably gentle
STUDENICA, ĆUPRIJA   and frankly unbewildered
                as eyes of village children
long before Giotto walked under the arcades of Padua
and mixed their copied bluenesses into Italian plaster;
Danitsé delivering your firstborn in the local maternity
clinic, sworn at by underpaid sadists masquerading
as uniformed midwives, possessed of the vilest and
most colourful proficiency in the art of rhetorical
abuse – *didn't you scream loud and long enough*
when he stuffed you senseless bitch so stuff
your moaning screaming whining bitching now;
Danitsé greeting new year as one of 500 guests
at the Mayor's reception for functionaries, among
hectares of Russian salad, mountains of meatballs
and 25 entire succulent spit-roasted suckling pigs
bordered by pastries, light-winged as hummingbirds;
KARABURMA   Danitsé, wiping greasy fingers
                and mouths of adored children,
nine years married, living with your mother-in-law
and her affable, passive, indecisive son, who
works harder than you but earns half as much,
ZVEZDARA   and two daughters by him
                in the two-roomed apartment
in a block where the lifts don't work, on the shabbier

side of town at the end of the shambling tramline;
Danitsé, arguing politics with brilliant impoverished
internationally informed taxi-drivers who steer

SLAVIJA   battered Fords and Mercedes in
                 bedroom slippers, owing to gout
or poverty or accident or God-Knows-What,
who offer unpredictably original opinions and

STUDENTSKI TRG   have given up smoking
                        unfiltered cigarettes and
possess IQ's of one hundred and seventy or eighty
and are local chess champions; Danitsé, preparing
squid-flavoured risottos that blacken the tongue
and oysters dressed in divine greenery for impromptu

SPLIT   song festivals among
                        Diocletian's palatial alleys;
Danitsé selling off four-volume sets of etymological
dictionaries that belonged to grandfather, browsing

KNEZ MIHAJLOVA   in second hand platonic
                        bookshops at the piazza-end
for German nineteenth century philosophical tracts
and English detective novels in Tauchnitz editions
and French symbolist poets bound in disintegrating

KOD KONJA   red leather, then eating ice cream by
                   the fountain near the equestrian statue;
Danitsé, knowing *not* to enquire but to keep very quiet
indeed when neighbours disappeared unaccountably;

ŠABAC, KLENAK, SAJMIŠTE   Danitsé whose three
                                 second cousins also
smoothly vanished overnight, never to be heard of
or mentioned again, not a peep; Danitsé finally
yourself entirely falsely accused by some anonymous
conniving swine of a two-faced lily-livered informer
who'd have sold or bartered his own mother or sister's
love-canal for the merest sniff of a sinecure or promotion,
the details of their charge of Jesus-Knows-What being

entirely immaterial, simply because at some point they
were bound to catch up with you on some trumped up
charge anyway; Danitsé arrested, cool early morning,
and taken off, quietly, in a canvas covered truck;
Danitsé barely surviving winter on Savage Island
GOLI OTOK, SVETI GRGUR   *aka* Naked Island *aka*
                                Barren Island, where
fellow prisoners perished for no reason or some
mildly ironic quip or anecdote told to the wrong
commissar; Danitsé not quite starving, skinny,
toughened up, through-and-past despairing,
more lightly moving, but always failing utterly
to self-censor fantasy of memories – or memory of
fantasies; Danitsé, divorced, returned, partly restored
POSTOJINSKA JAMA   to favour and employment as
                            official tour-guide in ghostly
whispering grottoes, escorting randy ambassadors
and distinguished foreign delegates on behalf of
regional commissariat for brotherhood and unity;
POSLEDNJA ŠANSA   Danitsé sipping coffee with
                        an ageing poet with cancer and
two months to live; Danitsé picking chrysanthemums;
Danitsé pickling cabbage leaves; Danitsé recalling but
trying *not* to recall the whole of your family feasting at
OHRID, ADA CIGANLIJA   the autumn equinox on
                         pink-fleshed lake trout
or white-fleshed river trout, chilled with crisp white
wine; Danitsé with a definite *tick*, even if barely
discernible to those who never knew you, an in-
voluntary minuscule squeezing at precisely each
third blink, of muscles around both eyes; Danitsé
quietened, inside and outside, talking about nothing,
deliberate and clinical in dumbing-down awareness
of clicks on the phone, as if nobody were listening,
as if you were still unwarily-unsuspecting-naive

innocuous-innocent-Danitsé-with-no-past-to-hide;
Danitsé keeping strength up on water, bread and salt
throughout the hard times, rationing out shares
with the old man upstairs, toothless, incontinent,
who once fought as a partisan and, next door,
the twin boys with mother working as a char;
Danitsé at the dentist, smoking, drinking coffee,
chatting to assistants and other queuing women
VRAČAR   waiting in turn to have
                                         fillings crammed
with something like silver, something like gold; fully
reinstated comrade Danitsé, one-time factory steward
whose younger comrades, taken on a decade later, have
managed to stand resolute before you in the everlasting
JURIJA GAGARINA   queue for a vacant eighth
                                         floor shoe-box apartment,
unless you were most improbably to decide to sleep
with the supervisor – just once, well, maybe twice,
as your own small personal contribution towards
the onward ongoing social struggle for a better life,
and so engineer yourself a couple of places forward,
which, you, being a lady, as well as a model citizen,
indeed would never dream of; more-than-ever
anxious Danitsé, muttering to yourself, *Look at you,
you scraggy old bag, he wouldn't want you anyway,*
now that you come to examine your defects, naked
in the mirror; mature sensible policy-making Danitsé,
still relatively high-breasted and slim-waisted, unable
to afford more than a black coffee in the canteen before
entering and sitting, smiling, throughout the inane
yawnworthy-jargon-crammed lecture by the latest
bald perspiring liberal Visiting Professor of Sociology
From Ohio or Oklahoma or Kentucky or Kansas or
God-Knows-Where, pontificating to the natives on
Obesity and Globalisation; tough, resolute Danitsé,

[11]

whose own younger sister at her wedding feast sang
VRANJE   songs all morning, afternoon
        and evening, well into the small
hours, and also led the dancing, whose groom
reverted to being a boor, scoundrel, gambler,
and, after six months of beatings, abandoned her
POŽAREVAC with child; Danitsé, paid to attend,
        as delegate for somewhere,
a major conference in the centre of nowhere
on future ramifications, central importances,
couched in officially sanctified periphrasis, at a
rundown hotel with rat poison under the wardrobe
in each identical room, and cockroaches in each basin,
where you drank sour coffees and brandy for breakfast
and smoked yourself senseless, like all other delegates,
PIROT   next to a factory for remoulding
        tyres, smelling of toasted
rubber; Danitsé, deputy director of God's own little
dream factory, where next to nothing has ever
worked, for no apparent reason, yet everything has
somehow half miraculously succeeded in carrying on
quite normally, even under alien occupiers, beneath
bombings, among ruins, and despite ineradicably
endemic bribery and corruption; confused hype-
and-multiple-propaganda-bombarded Danitsé
somehow sporting a fresh open mind, because
even though things couldn't be worse, they're just
bound to get better, *who knows, one day, some time,*
even if not quite yet, aren't they; Danitsé ever ready
for active service in the loyal pursuit of dreamworlds;
Danitsé, cursed and blest with unrealisable futurities;
Danitsé of dramatic nostalgias and deep-seated conditionals
embedded in longings for stable and certain histories;
Danitsé whose centres are always edges and frontiers
of somewhere else, of someone else's aspirations,

somebody else's powers; good-neighbourly Danitsé
of inflated suspicions and conspiracy theories; flawless
perfectionist Danitsé of many faults, mostly blamed
on others, rarely on yourself; Danitsé believing or at
least prepared to believe, almost wholeheartedly, in
the refashioning of hope, refurbishment of the real,
furtherance of the possible, transparency of justice,
boundlessness of fortune, depthlessness of joy and
ineffable, unassailable dignity of wisdom and love;
Danitsé, proficient in two alphabets for one language;
TERAZIJE   ageless Danitsé, demonstrating,
                              singing and laughing
nose-to-nose in the front line with students one third
your own age facing baton-and-water-cannon-bearing
SKUPŠTINA   police backed by tanks and
                              tear gas beneath graceless
statues to moustachioed sabre-bearing heroes who
would rather die than surrender to any enemy, ever;
many-times betrayed Danitsé, whose own godforsaken
SREBRENICA   sons have harried, hunted, rooted out,
                     incarcerated, tortured, crippled, mown
down and, in fields, lanes and woodland ditches left
grandparents, godparents – whole families – to rot;
Danitsé, ousted from your village, whose retaliating
KRAJINA   grandsons, in spurious names
                             of necessity, revenge, honour,
have shot at, raided, pillaged and re-occupied the house
you were lucky to get away from, just in time; refugee
Danitsé, both adoring and hurtful to those who love you
but bitterest of all to those of your own blood; Danitsé
descended from lost tribes on plains and hills and by
rivers hollowed out of the bowl of God-Knows-Where
way back beyond the Carpathians and the Urals, now
dispersing to Australia, Argentina, Canada, California
and other maybe blander but even yet more faceless

God-Knows-Wheres, where still everything seems
possible or, rather *did* seem, at least from far-off,
before departure; Danitsé who, thanks to excellent
connections, did manage to find a job abroad, but
couldn't stick it, no way, and had to come back
home to a home no longer *home*; Danitsé stuck for
good among provincial snobs and backbiting gossips
including ancient spinsters who would drink pure acid
rather than reveal their own personal secrets to a single
stranger; Danitsé, menopausal, with incipient arthritis,
barren Danitsé, intent on mothering orphans;
Danitsé, cancer-ridden, still surviving somehow;
Danitsé, toothless concierge and sweeper of dust
from church floors, flattener and comber of sand-trays
for spindly yellow candles perched on wooden tripods, loyal
filler of holy oils in incense-burners that dangle from right
arms of forgotten forefather priests, swinging across
these present times, like pendula in slow motion;
Danitsé, with hope in your heart, even these days . . .

while this spring's nightingales, as in every other,
are drowning out the hum of overhanging galaxies,
so stark in their radiance, and insufferably bright,
they appear about to fall, even though they're receding

. . . these days – why is it you look and sound like
everybody else; or have you cloned, or disguised
yourself, or even taken vows, disappeared into
a convent that never grants visits, grows its own
carrots and lettuces, keeps goats, geese and chickens
fenced in by reedbeds and pollarded willows, on one
of those little islands on a backwater of the river
that scarcely anyone notices; or, Danitsé, have you
thumbed a lift from the long-striding captain of
a big river barge, not to be dropped off till you

reach the eastern sea, or have you decided,

NEBESNA   simply, to float off finally

                and forever angelic into

a cloudless sky, seeing that I at least can't trace
you at home or anywhere and currently no longer
have an inkling how to find you in the morning?

2   By the Banks of the Sava

Eight Memorial Tablets

Memories of the days I spent in the camp have haunted me throughout the past sixty years, most of all at nighttime. I have often started writing about them, but each time gave up, because it meant experiencing their horrors all over again.

Fear that the truth will go with me to the grave has given me the strength to write this book in my old age. I hope that it will contribute to preventing anything similar happening again.

CADIK I. DANON BRACO

The hands that mowed them down remain unknown.
The river has moved on. The grass has grown.
By the banks of the Sava, Death was their plough.
Whatever their names were, honour them now.

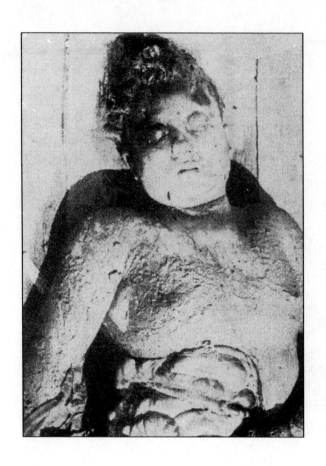

Promise was hers, and sight of sun and stars.
O Lord of Heaven, or your Avatars,
What explanation? Or analysis?
She should have had a better chance. Not this.

No, she is not Ophelia, but a Jew
or Serb. She could have been me or you.
Her body floated down the Sava River.
This epitaph is all I have to give her.

They might as well have tied them up in sacks.
Instead they tied their hands behind their backs.

Apart from the sick and foetid smell,
when left in water, corpses swell.
Tongues fill mouths to the velar vault.

This was their fate but not their fault.
People with voices and spirit, like you,
bring parsley, fennel, rosemary, rue.

These are the folk who really call the shots,
a bunch of ordinary have-nots.
Don't master murderers always find such berks,
grinning and servile, to do their dirty works?

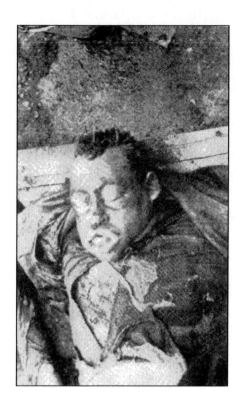

Here's Engineer Rosenberg pulled from the well.
Bring poppies, agapanthi, asphodel.

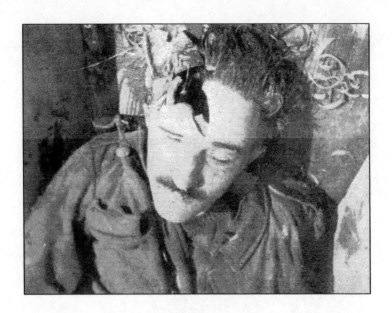

He was dead when they broke into his head.
and now his skull lies uninhabited.
Did his murderers mean to shatter his soul,
pour that out, too, through the gaping hole?
Flown here, his soul calls: *Murdering fails.*
And, over Death, his great soul prevails.

3   Under Balkan Light

mi dva

Language doesn't, languages don't
cope with this kind of thing all that
often or well. So what this really is
about and after is to do with what
tends to fall out of and away from
words and fails to get trapped in their
nets. In Slovenian there exists a 'fourth
person singular' that opposes the
deathful *He* and means the intimate
small case *you* plus *I*, you and me, as
if we were one, as one: *mi dva*, us two,
the-two-of-us-as-one. Even though that
condition can't be expressed or even
intimated in *this* grammar, aren't all
languages, all of us (*nous autres,
noi altri*), ready for *mi dva*? What this
is about and after again and always
is standing on tiptoe right on top of
whatever grounds and cónstructs may
be available for support, and stretching
and reaching up and out for a touch
and possibly, hopefully, even for a hold and
grasp that have not quite yet happened
to or in *any* language. This is what being
under Balkan light continuously
is and is about and again and
again keeps provoking and calling
and making flickeringly present.

Seagull's wings

For an instant
beating
seagull's wings

take up the whole
sky. This heaven-
filling happens

both at zenith and nadir
of their pulsing and
drumming on wind.

Time, unstitched
from history, goes
into reverse. At the

ferry's stern we stand,
so wholly held by this
watching, that distances

slip into haze. Everything
broken is mended. Where we
are is the horizon.

Notes from three cities

A WALLET

I left the cab on Vašintonova Street, not knowing my wallet had fallen from my pocket on the seat next to the driver, just after I had paid him. Ten minutes later, by cruising, he found me walking the spaces of his city, map in hand, half dreaming. He hooted me, rolled down his window, and with scarcely grin or wink, leaned out to hand back my worn leather holder of notes, snaps, mementoes – my precious personal scraps of history and identity. *Here*, he said, *take it*. And he thrust it into my hands, changed gears and revved away. In the ensuing silence, the light became crystal, and I recalled his eyes, momentarily blazing, *I recognise you.*

White cherries

The woman was heavily pregnant and should have taken a cab. The tower block they lived in was three kilometres from Zemun. *I'm going out*, she called to her partner, *to the market to buy white cherries*. She returned three hours later carrying several kilos. *You might have had an accident*, he said. *I walked*, she said, and laughed, *There weren't any cabs anyway*.

FISH SOUP

Rainy Sunday, on the uncertain border of Spring. My old friend was visiting me from England with his new wife. He wanted to take her to Smederevo, to show her a restaurant famous for fish soup, which he'd stopped at on his way to Greece, twenty years or more before. So we drove off from Belgrade, found the place without difficulty, and ordered, just as it was getting dark. We were the first customers to arrive. A gypsy fiddler sat smoking, waiting for the clientele. Over our *šlivovice*, I mentioned to my friends some lines of an Old Town Song, and hummed them. The gypsy overheard, stubbed out his cigarette, came over to our table and, without any comment or by-your-leave, played and sang it for us, verse by haunting verse . . . *Ima dana kada ne znam šta da radim* . . . The fiddle and his voice re-opened separate wounds stored in each of our memories, took them out, re-examined them, and bound them back tight inside us on the instrument's chords. The constant reiteration of this kind of sudden invasive intervention from totally unexpected quarters constitutes the specific quality of light in the Balkans.

On the qualities of light in the Balkans

Smederevo

Between skin and core of apple
lies the secret. And in the taste of grape
before its flesh is broken. At the shore
of daylight pounded by waves of evening
darts the unseen arrow, and on the slope of first or last light
against a doorframe or window rests the cutting edge,
as if honed on a millstone high above the clouds
to stab directly down through silver rivers of sky.

In the window, as if etched, the reflection of a face
I have not seen before, glances back familiarly.
It is neither yours nor mine. It is neither
living nor dead. It corresponds to neither zone.
It belongs alone to this light it is intimately part of.
And the smile on this face, which is not exactly a smile,
belongs to a white angel, with darkening, bluetipped wings.

Entry is not so difficult, although always unexpected.
Here is a blue butterfly, arrested on your finger
at the gate to the site of a massacre. Here is a spider's web
dewflecked in a morning garden. And here
a hint of incense suspended among dust
in a deserted building. Its silence is a song
launched on the space between separated trays
of candles lit for the living and the dead.
And here, the frayed hem fringed around a shadow
that penetrates deep into it across the porous borders
drilled into time by ancestors and survivors.

And there, under the shadow of the ruined fortress
where we stood one evening beside a windless river
between the pearled moon and its hollowed reflection
is the poor death of stillness, pierced by nothing more
than a pebble skimmed across water by a casual boy.
And here, after all is said, is the certain chime of light
from eye to eye, as glass rings against glass.
So take this wine and drink it.

Poem at the Autumn Equinox

Returning dreams. The one about falling
and the one about a house
owned and lived in but never fully explored
and the one containing a word
clearly heard and recognised
from a language unknown,
which I can never pronounce. Now you have gone
let them take me over. I am their island
willing to be drowned.

After the end of falling, you will come to a river
and walk beside it along a worn footpath
bordered by nettles and willows.
In the house you will find a room
and in the room a mirror,
and in the mirror a portrait of a girl dressed in leaves,
golden and green, and in her hand a wand.
After the word and the deaths of its many echoes
first you will hear a silence strike like a gong
and then from the silence another voice emerge,
and that is the voice to listen to,
that is the voice to follow. The girl
who enters the room and looks out of her mirror
stands on the tide and her wand is the rainbow.

The voice arrives on the tide but is no part of it
and if it seems to belong wholly to the sea
or if it seems to belong wholly to the wind
or if its substance seems partially made of cloud,
reflections, falling leaves, or invisible splinters of light,
do not be mistaken by the sweetness of appearances.

The path leads to cliffs where butterflies and bees
play all summer long, and night is full of stars.
The girl who stands on the tide against a white horizon.
has turned into a willow framed against the sky,
and her wand which was the rainbow has spiralled away

on wings, migrating south for winter. Nothing is left
but emptiness – except for the voice. And the voice
cannot stop singing now, and all you have to do
is burn its sound in your heart and treasure it there forever.

Fragment: on *The Sepharad*

'And as Obadiah had foretold, the Jews who had been exiled from the Holy City of Jerusalem would find refuge in the *Sepharad*. And it came to pass that in the golden peninsula of Iberia, to the far west of the Great Middle Sea, which later came to be known as Spain and Portugal, they received due and fitting welcome. And there they settled and prospered for hundreds of years, dwelling in peace with their neighbours and excelling not only in all branches of learning, scholarship and healing, but also in the civil arts of counselling, negotiation and diplomacy, the higher metaphysical arts of mathematics, astronomy and music, and those hidden arts enshrined in the *Zohar*, whereof it behoves not to speak in this account. And there they built temples of a splendour matched only by the ancient Temple of Solomon, and became proficient in strange tongues, of a beauty unparalleled by any other than the language of Hebrew itself. And some, alas, forgot the divinely ordained language of their origins among those alien melodies. Yet, in generation after generation, the lot of this people is Exile, and there came a day when the rulers of the golden land, as in Egypt of old, sought lambs to appease the wrath of the Almighty, and issued new decrees against the Jews, forcing them either outwardly to embrace the official faith and doctrines of that land, or to be expelled.

～

And thus, from the *Sepharad* itself, once more they set out on their wanderings, to the east and the north and the northeast, back along the shores of the Great Middle Sea, and deep into the dark heart of the continent of Europe, even as far as the Northern ocean, and beyond. And with them they took as a comfort and an inheritance the sweet and melodic language which their centuries of prosperity, peace and fortune in the *Sepharad* had engrafted so firmly upon their spirits, and its sap flowed through their very souls and ripened on their tongues in speech and in songs. And in their new exile, whether among adherents of Jesus or Mohammed, they became known to the world as the *Sephardim*, and the name of that language was Ladino.'

SALAMON RUBEN BEN ISRAEL OF SALONIKA, 1688

In war: June 4, 1943

Hampstead General Hospital: 7.25, to Rosalind
   née Schneiderman (anglicised to Taylor),
wife of Alexander Israel Berengarten,
   their firstborn son: Schloime Reuven.
BBC Home Service: 7.55, Lift Up Your Hearts.
   9.25, Songs of the River and Sea.
12.00, Russian Songs. 3.00, Music While You Work.
   9.20, The Electron Microscope.

> *In human isolation, the troops and wounded*
> > *were encased in a grim and closed world*
> *of their own, haunted by a new and demoralizing*
> > *Enemy – the ghost of hunger.*
> *The last herd of cattle, which in April had been*
> > *driven up the plateau from the Sandžak*
> *had been slaughtered, and the last remaining rations*
> > *distributed to the wounded, and fighting units.*

Cook wanted for Anglesey. Gentleman's house.
   Help given in kitchen. Exempt from
National Service and accustomed war-time cooking.
   Address P66 'M/C Guardian'. Clifford Turner,
Shoe Specialist, 46 King Street, Manchester,
   Closed for Whitsun. Lecture, 8. p.m. Friday,
N.E.C. Centre: 'Should Antisemitism Be Made
   a Crime?' D. N. Pritt, K.C., M.P.

Fifteen to twenty deaths were recorded daily
in the hospital columns. By 3 June the plan
for a central evacuation of the wounded
had to be abandoned. Only three surviving
doctors were working with the Supreme Staff.
The silent column of the disbanded hospitals
stretched, in dumb anticipation, for fifty miles
across the naked heights between the rivers.

One union for the coal industry, with 600,000 miners
as members, is now a practical possibility.
Five salesgirls at Bourne & Hollingsworth protested
at having to wear silk stockings on duty.
Five German officers and NCOs rounded up in Tunisia
did not know the campaign was over. All wore
the Iron Cross, including the youngest, aged sixteen.
Thousands of women will work in the shipyards.

A brutal decision was taken. The serious casualties
were to be hidden in caves and undergrowth
on the steep slopes of the Piva: the lightly wounded
were to be escorted by the Seventh Division
to the north-west; and the remainder, who formed
the main group, protected by the Third Division,
were ordered to force a passage to the south-east
back across the Tara to the Sandžak.

BBC Forces Network: 8.20, Music of Gaelic Scotland.
12.00, Geraldo and His Orchestra.
6.40, Some Famous Spy Stories. 8.30, Tommy Trinder.
Rainy; cool, with fresh south-westerly wind,
strong at times; sea choppy; low ceiling of cloud;
visibility deteriorating. De Gaulle and Girard
form Government of Freedom. Blackout: 10.54 p.m.
to 5.02 a.m. Moon sets 11.23 p.m. rises 8 a.m.

*Movement began on the night of 4–5 June, and in
the succeeding fateful days, all central direction
evaporated. The road to the Sandžak was closed.
New wounded reached the Central Hospital daily.
Orders of the Supreme Command to hide the worst wounded
in the Piva caves could not be carried out.
There was neither contact with the local population
nor time: only 'the convulsions which precede death'.*

Theatres: A Month in the Country. The Dancing Years.
520 Soviet Planes Bomb Orel. Heartbreak House.
Night bombs on Birmingham, Fareham, Eastbourne.
The Merry Widow. Arsenic and Old Lace.
Cinemas: Ritz Leicester Square, Gone With the Wind.
Regal Marble Arch, Casablanca. Tatler
Charing Cross Road, Lenin in 1918. Ambassador
Hendon, When Johnny Comes Marching Home.

June 8 was the worst night of the war. The tracks
were blocked by stretchers and these cases
were left to their fate. In one unit the numbers
of troops and wounded could be counted
only by sections of bark torn from the beech trees
for 'nourishment' along the mountain trail.
The Warsaw Ghetto had fallen. Four days later, in
Golders Green, Schloime Reuven was circumcised.

Memorial tablet for Lili Böhm

This is the hanging of Lily Böhm,
Jewess, martyr, patriot.
She deserved better than she got
and more than this poor requiem.

Memorial tablet for a slave labourer

Forced labourer, Bor silver mine.
They forced him to wear the slave sign,
then shot him. Earth received his blood.
But see, a star can shine from mud.

Poem at the Spring Equinox

Dreams I would wish away. The one about a child
being attacked and tortured, everybody helpless,
me most of all. And the one where we run and run
and our breaths and strides
    along the coastline under summer stars
        seem at first to harmonise
            with wind and waves
but we never quite make it, because they always
come after us, prise us from our hiding places,
        haul us off for questioning
against gunshots and wailing.

            And the dream
      about the trench
          hidden
          at the edge of a field
behind two hillocks, one a mud covered heap
of excavated slag, the other a growing pile
of clothes and shoes, and the long trench
a grave, squirming like an ant heap, packed
      with people, some still groaning,
          lying higgledy-piggledy
      over one another.

    I want to call out,

      It's not just their bodies
        but souls
     being destroyed here

but nothing comes out of my mouth, not
            a breath,
not a grunt, not a scream.

            And it's us
being marched towards that ditch, us standing
naked over it, crouching, vomiting, drooling,
        us falling down into it.

        Us the ones. Us.

2

Day unfolds like a blanket smothering the kingdom
of darkness. But the papery texture of light
is too flimsy to last and its undercurrents
too turbulent. Again tomorrow night
                        this coverlet of mine
will be devoured by the small precise teeth
of starving invisible rodents that steadily gnaw
        at the thin canvas of consciousness
            tent pegs of morality
                tautened ropes of hope
                    groundsheets tossed over despairs
and the thwarted monsters redouble their previous fury.

Dreams like movie clichés. Dreams I am hooked on
like nicotine or speed. Dreams that made someone a bomb.
Dreams of the twentieth century. Dreams of primordial
        visceral terror. Dreams of facts that are
                                true facts. Lord,
                    if you are there
or, if not, at least some henchman marginally
            rational,
                responsible,
take them from me, all of them.

3

Blossoms may indeed
be relied on
to perform their annual coronations,
fit out the trees in festive regalia,
and the zephyr's mouth be filled
with perfumed flowers like candy

but now the snows have broken, the tanks
have been remobilised and last year's raw recruits
have already been trained up
into this year's crack battalions.

4

But in other dreams
     lurks a child

          neither image nor part-image

     nor fleeting shadow in cloud

          nor shape glimpsed among leaves
               or through reflections in water

     nor patterned in surfaces
          of dolomite or basalt

who has not been formed or born

          has not yet descended

     remains unglimpsed through the eye
          of the fourth person singular

          nor rests
          gift of the wind
               blown mote or dust speck
          on the i of the deepest sigh
nestled in a mother's longing

nor meristem on the highest
          leaf-tip at the tree-top
     of a father's yearning

5

Who'll hear this
across the barricaded years?

not a prophet
still less an Avatar

Enough of Saviours
All of them deceive

a human child –
miraculous enough

And should that child appear
in sleeping or waking

what is
to be done?

Track
circle
backtrack
follow

Poem for my infant daughter
   at Mileševa Monastery

1

My daughter, two months old,
we have driven you across the borders of seven countries
to ring this monastery bell on an August Sunday
to wait in its privet-scented garden
with a cat sprawled asleep on a flowerbed,
a hen, a turkey, a flock of sheep and a peacock

for the keeper, this young black-bearded monk,
gaunt, high cheekboned, to open his basilica door
so we might ask blessing
of the resident angel of Mileševa.

2

Under your eyes, blue angel of Mileševa
I stand before you with a daughter,
my *božidar*, blessing in middle age,

who, even as she tumbled from her mother
in that first instant of air and independent being,
was formed so perfect, we recognised –

as if a spore of radiance threaded on a light beam
had sparked breath in the grosser stuff of matter
for her life-dawn – that she had been made since always.

3

Child, you are not yet aware
around your infancy rage
millennial hope and despair.

and has it been foreseen
your life will span two ages
and you a borderer between?

Your sleeping eyes I kiss.
May the wisdom of these sages
keep you from all distress

and hold you above hopelessness
and protect you from perfidiousness
and not yield you to unhappiness.

4

White angel, secret guardian
of the secret gardens of Yugoslavia,
you who see through and through
the tellings of lies and time –

smile on my infant daughter.
guard her and guide her, white angel.

Poem for a very small child

Hushabye and close
your eyes and breathe
gently now because

the ant's strong legs
will bear you into sleep
the back of a butterfly

transport you and
the breath of a bird
blow you high

away into dreamland where
you'll roll on cloud
then tumble and fall

pearled in a raindrop
onto the glossy blade
of a hart's tongue fern

and there you'll slumber
until morning peels
away night's drapes

Father to small child

I am your tent, a membrane made
of tissue ribbed and wrapped in flesh,
and thoughts and dreams, a finer mesh
on which imprints of stars are laid.

Under the storm I toss and turn,
under the wind I flap and sway,
you fill me as light fills the day,
under the sun I swell and burn.

Rest in me, gypsy soul, in calm.
I am the rest upon your way,
I am your nest though the trees sway.
Come to no tears or pain or harm.

The soul is vaporous mist, sea haze,
fistfuls of water, light, and praise,
sunflecks at noon, heart's ease
and evenings under palm trees.

Borderers

1. BORDERERS

In those days, we
travelled light, took
few possessions.

Preferring tortuous
mountain passes to
trodden ways

across plain, or by river,
we spurned highroads
and marked frontiers.

Today we remain
borderers, go-betweens,
our languages always

dialects, our eyes wary
in half-light, attentive
in dark to seven senses,

our ears alert, taking in
more than ever our
bland expressions let on.

2. RESIDENT GHOSTS

We are the edge-folk,
the end-and-beginning
people, suspicious of

unstated intentions in
voice behind voice,
glance beneath glance,

word undeclared by
self-declared friend, charm
of hostess, tactic of proven

and trusted ally, agenda
of respected colleague,
motive of best-disposed

neighbour. Captains,
remember, we are called
on, called for, called away

by resident ghosts in your
futures, and at all times
are ready to leave.

3. AUDITORS

Cunning in contest and
devious in battle, in some
things we never cheat, for

we are 'people of the book'
too. We keep our accounts
as carefully with the gods,

our gods, that is, as
with men. Auditors
of actual and impossible

numbers, peering in
sand grains, through
ashes, in dust, we scry

vaster darknesses
to sieve and track
from time's tendrils

minuscule miracles
and to map origins
and ends of light.

4. LONGING

Over the world, what
the songs sing of is
pain, lamentation, exile –

gust-blown travellers,
migrants in hope
all on the move

to and from different
zones, different voices,
the same song,

the same plangent
tone and expression,
the same longing

and the same yearning,
for a heavenly space
in the deep mind,

a home familiar in the quiet
heart, a single welcoming
face in the soul.

5. Elsewheres

Things have a habit
of accumulating elsewheres
or otherwise dissolving them.

Things accrue sediment
of memories. Then
they, or we, die.

But we, boarders,
borderers,
go hunting

an unnamed creature
that stands clear
from its surroundings

no matter where it finds
itself, in and among
things. We too prefer those

elsewheres. To run
with that creature
on a field of sky.

6. Now I confess

Now I confess – what
I want is nothing
other than this

small pack I carry
home this path that takes
me where I have to go

home itself being
the way itself
and path itself

path on the path
way on the way
way of sky and way of stone

way of oak and way of leaf
way of hammer and rainbows
way of air and fire

home this curious
journey full
of unexpected mornings

By the Danube, Zemun

New Year 1990

Curious, the fresh dead are knocking at the windows,
of our fourth floor flat on Gheorghe Gheorgiu-Dej Street,
hands scrabbling vainly with splintery nails of frost,
mouths pressed to the panes, clouding them with mist,
still too close to our world to be willing to let go.

Mostly, we are deaf to the dead, but this winter solstice
their volume can't be turned down. Nor can our ears
block away their din, in this rattle of panes on wind
from Timişoara, Arad, Şibiu, Braşov, Cluj, Bucureşti
howling westward across the Danube.

All our channels stay open. Ghosts against our screen,
crushed tens of thousands deep, are clamouring for breath,
vision, fire, return. Wide eyes too numb to protest
gaze on us through snowfall in the hopeless adoration
of ragged frozen children at dummies in a clothes store.

We wanted rest this winter but the world will not let us
pause or sit back an instant. Its borders, like snows, are
shifting, melting, refreezing. The millennium approaches.
Deformed or unformed, living and unborn call Justice
and all our human dead belong to us, all, being human.

Leave these windows open, that the fallen of Romania
may range through our home, guide and command
this breath, occupy uncensored stations of this voice,
and these words, wholly theirs, nourish their welcome
presences, as cleanly as your milk blesses our child.

To Zora

Which one of us has escaped, Zora, you or me,
out of this mire we've both found ourselves in,
And if into exile, where? We've lived in and through
each other's company so long, our breaths have frosted
and throats parched in so many seasons, our features
grown so similar, whatever happens to either of us
only one thing is sure: we'll carry each other's images
like photographs in the passports of our souls.

Once, remember, we scarcely had need to talk,
and because we knew each other's thoughts anyway
the merest glance was enough to say everything.
Or so I thought. Was that *my* illusion? When you stole
away one night on a secret assignment with death
firmly believing I knew and suspected nothing,
you didn't spot me watching you from the window
hammering useless fists against the walls.

Throughout that night I lay wide-eyed till dawn
feigning sleep only when I heard your key
scrape the gullet of a sombre morning. *You
foreigners know nothing and will never understand,*
you said after showering, as you blew
hot air through your hair. Zora, full of boloney,
I no longer have answers to any of your questions
and neither do you, to any one of mine.

Guests

Yes, we have come for rest, so
give us, kindly, rest's instruments –
salt, bread, dried fruit, olives,
a little meat if you have it,
and a flask of local wine.
We have no needs or preferences
especially out of the ordinary,
no special news, imports, nothing
to declare or purvey. Only let
your basins be clean, cushions
freshly aired, sheets spotless
and cool, couches without vermin.
We do have our own obligations,
that is, several duties and rituals
which incidentally require of us
certain minor observances –
concerning which however we really
need not trouble you. Nor shall
we dream of burdening you
with more than conventional courtesies
in thanks for your unobtrusive
kindly hospitality, and no, of course,
absolutely, no trinkets, no gifts,
no mementoes, let alone any such
subtler outlandish embarrassments
as unredeemable blessings.
We assure you we shall pack
away our utensils neatly
leaving no traces of them.
We shall rise early, pay and be gone.
Dawn's shadows will efface us
and by noon we shall have left
no ripple on the surface of memory.

4 The Voice in the Garden

Who can I ask about the voice in the gardens?

IVAN V. LALIĆ

It's painful and difficult, the living are not enough for me
First because they do not speak, and then
Because I have to ask the dead
In order to go on farther.

GEORGE SEFERIS

Whose voice?

A scarecrow hanging in wardrobe or cupboard
calls from a jacket you've not worn in years.
Whose is that cry from the edge of the keyboard
that even your trained inner ear hardly hears,
seamless yet seeming, buttoning holes
of silence in speech? On whose shirt, the soul's?
   Whose is that call that escapes where it chooses
   but when you want it to come back, refuses?

In the kitchen, beneath the whirr of the drier,
the leaky tap's drip, or rattle in pipes,
on the phone, behind the known voice on the wire,
crackling on sound tracks, whining through tapes –
whose is that voice on the verges of hearing
you know but don't know, that keeps disappearing,
   with a sound, not a sound, as of waves breaking
   over margins between sleeping and waking?

In a café, behind the hum and the racket,
whose throat owns that voice, familiar, far fetched?
In an ashtray, scrawled on some cigarette packet
in invisible ink, indelibly etched,
who wrote that message you don't understand
but strive to repeat here? What's shaking your hand?
   Beyond ultra-violet, beneath infra-red,
   who sewed irridescent song in your head?

Who can I ask

... about the voice in the gardens?

Not certainty, to shape your ways of going
on well-made roads, to take you where you're due,
not trust, the deepest form of inner knowing
whatever happens, somehow you'll get through.
Not hope, frail bridge across the flooded river
you stand beside, too wide, too deep to ford,
not even love, the gift that is its giver,
nor faith in works of humans, or The Lord.
Not profit or approval, prize or gain,
not honours, favours, fame, advancements, offices,
not cure, or even brief respite, from pain,
Not promises, not formulas, not prophecies.
The voice reveals itself and that is all
and that it is at all is miracle.

The voice in the garden

Did you ask for apotheosis, or transcendence,
or something else, not either, yet still higher,
when that curious voice assailed you in the garden
with song, unearthly, that you could not fully
comprehend in origin or depth, but knew
and recognised for what it was – a miracle
woven out of the silences, the pauses,
gaps and gulfs between perfumes, colours, movements,
or grace abundant, superimposed on grace –
realising the voice inside your head,
wired into time, earthed, forking out through space,
was the living call to the unborn from the dead?

The dead themselves need no miracles. They are
what we shall once become, when we have learned
our final lesson: that to stand alone
is the only genuine source of grace, or love,
particularly that most human one
that can deny itself for another's happiness,
besides which, all else is mere need, or appetite
ephemeral nature thrusts our silly hearts in.
The dead know being in love is the good glue
that sticks together beings to form a true
union of nothings within everything.
That is the open secret you heard sing.

Lovers who gaze into each other's eyes
and smile, awake, as body enters body,
devouring passion's core in toothed embrace
deep through the face of otherness, to their interior
impossible mirroring space of mutual bliss,
may snatch a chord or chorus of that song
if they are attentive to its timelessness
coursing through both and each, quiet, passionless.
The glue of physical love will crack, and hope,
regret, fear, longing, lease them a long rope
for skipping, hanging or imprisonment.
Was this, then, all that subtle singing meant?

Say, isn't every secret worth its keeping
as open-hearted, generous and full-throated
in outpouring, as the choir of these dumb trees
you walk among here, hearing, overhearing
their aweful and tremendous joys and sadnesses
lifted on the ripening of your discovery
that deepest root and leaf tip read one score
to sing this air delivered by no single
voice you can identify or grasp?
We fear what we can't recognise or clasp,
but what we love is more mysterious still.
Deepest familiarity breeds miracle.

Spilling out from itself, all singing is
what cannot be contained, the singular glory
of being, itself, its own apotheosis
which needs ask nothing, nothing being all it holds,
nor is there pattern that does not transcend
its own form's pure perfection and its radiant
immanence in the merest fact of calling
or being called, being perceived, being made
manifest, recognised, seen, heard, loved, believed.
Things wear each other's cores just as they dress
themselves in strange appearance. What's perceived
as essence is the sheen of otherness.

So, Ivan, as you listen in your garden,
you know we, living, are a double skein
of bass and treble, padlock, key and chain
that link and loose the unborn and the dead,
nor do you need to ask them for the ways
of going, who rest peaceful in their graves,
in dust, in fire. But do not be mistaken:
the dead have not gone elsewhere. They are here
inside us, in the song. This is its sense.
We are their audience and the instruments
they play on, who conduct all living things
as willing pipe and horn and shimmering strings.

Everything, even suffering, is a gift.
Everything made, unmade, or not yet made
is grist to the mill of poetry and fortune
we turn and turn on, reined, its willing slaves.
For you, who've dowsed and fathomed faintest sounds
that hatch through cracks of timelessness in time,
to mine, in merely mortal song, a vein
spilt from the eternal – I ask this:
that in your singing, even pain be blessed,
and every shell, cell, pebble, dustspeck, spore,
sandflower crystal or pearl nucleus, best
become itself, true miracle, to the core.

In the mirror

Voices in the mirror call
The commonplace is miracle.

Hill of the Fountains

A string of fountains down the hillside. Rilled terraces and
tended vines of pearly muscatel. Carved into the slope, like
steps. Built up as layered soilbeds

And protected from weathers' ravages by ancient drystone walls.
Trimmed neat and bright as children's beds. As if by a
friendly giant from a fable.

And below it, on the valley's far side, as I zigzag down, a village
whose wines are headier than any grown in my own country.
I long to roll their flavours on my tongue.

This is a place where the air itself is sweet. It collects in greater
densities to absorb even more freshness. It rushes out to
greet me, as I approach the fountains.

Here I have come to ask for peace. To plead for it. With nobody,
except myself alone. I shall stay tonight at the village inn.
And, in the morning, go walk the Hill of the Fountains.

The stork

You stand on the roof of a single storeyed house and watch the
   stork leave her nest. Her huge ungainly wings take finicky
   stabs at the air. But now she is high,

Slow-battering the currents. In control. You've no idea where
   she's heading. She's travelling higher, west over the plain,
   not east over

the mountain. In all directions the limpid light turns all things
   you see to nakedness. The sky has no trace of cloud. She gets
   smaller and smaller. Now she is a V

and now a flattened line. No hint of haze on this morning air.
   But despite your intense attention, she melts away from your
   vision before she hits any horizon.

The garment of death

The garment of death is a shedding of all garments,
woven from gaps in thought and rents in meditation,
lacerations in waves, holes in dew-decked spiders' webs,
spaces torn out of memory and silences from music,
gashes in breath and rips in understanding.

The garment of death is invisible and unsayable
even to its most accomplished tailors and couturiers.
The garment of death is unwearable on this side
of the one-way mirror our detached guardian angels
watch us through as they play dice or cards for us.

The garment of death is the stripping of all seven
layerings of soul-veils from the body of the bride
and the piercing of the ultimate of all her virginities.
The garment of death is the nakedness of the bridegroom
when he has finally worn his body inside out.

The garment of death is made of the unmaking
of sheer light by dark, of dark devoured by light,
a net, opaque, transparent, a reflecting and shimmering
vestment worn by fire for the honouring of dust
and by dust for the transformation into nothing of fire.

When time is gnawed by perfection in the very act of love,
the garment of death, buttoned by heavenly stars,
seamed by impervious void and patched with a little air,
is the robe we have stolen, or borrowed for a while,
from compound ancestries and multiple posterities.

Poem for Andjelka

Going down with cancer and no space left
on the page of your life for much more writing
no space left in your lungs for much more breathing
no space left in your sky for any more stars

Ned Goy has gone out

Through solar hub and stellar rim
Ned has gone out on the same long limb
accorded Hebrews and Goyim.

He has gone out like a huffed candle
blown through the door with no handle
with Hun, Illyrian and Vandal,

Vlach, Rom, Slav, Celt, Turk and Greek –
he saw through all, unproud, unmeek,
valued all, knew when to speak

and when to practise thrust and cut,
parry or feint with *if* or *but*
and when to keep his mouth shut.

Now he has gone out, universal,
where no split blessing, prayer or curse'll
foster longing or reversal.

Black mountain wolf and English falcon,
tiger-hearted burning Balkan,
there's no more listening or talking

late through the night, burnt cigarettes,
emptied whiskies, singing, bets,
spurnings of lies, cants, etiquettes,

correctnesses in fad and fashion,
jungle law, unreason, ration –
just no more of your wit and passion

clear in intellectual quest
for forms to wreak out justice best.
Ned, lay down your head now. Rest.

Great-hearted and fun-loving friend,
nothing can resurrect or mend
those times now, at their natural end.

To write simply again

To write simply again
is what the heart requires
from the gap left by pain
and embers from fires.

To think simply once more
is what the mind demands
from the pips in the core
and tired gnarled hands.

And to rest safe at last
is what the soul craves
from the last chill blast
of brass over graves.

Tonight the war ended

Tonight the war ended
and a small grey and silver flecked moth
sitting in my bathroom basin
moved on to my hand and patiently waited
for me to open the window
and let him out on the street
into summer darkness

I dreamed I slept

I dreamed I slept, and in that sleep I dreamed,
and from that double dream interior woke
and walked in a closed courtyard. Someone spoke
behind me, and I turned. A dark girl beamed
brown eyes at me. I gazed. 'Just as you seemed
in dream to dream, so by the double stroke
of waking into waking, from this yoke
you've shouldered, may you be redeemed.'
So when I enter my last mortal sleep,
after all dreams have gone, and I am dead,
will then I wake and, doubly waking, keep
some mirror of that garden in my head
and, back inside it, rising from the deep
distress of death, sleepwalk? Or wake instead?

Bogomil

Whether a hinted half-traced face appears
sudden in dark or light, from the last wave
of grief that beat and carved onto this grave
some message that might mock oncoming years,
like *Rest In Peace*, in spite of mourners' tears –
or whether doubt, dread, terror made them rave
because from nothing, they might nothing save
of sweet life and its sultry atmospheres –
if you could scry that face, might you then give
meanings back to lost symbols spelt upon
summers in Sumer or in Babylon,
and so, by tracing serifs, sift or sieve
in nets of light, worlds still to come, or gone,
or snatch them through dark glass, in negative?

Night, Summer

Summer radiance again, among the unkempt gardens
outside the shuttered window, willows by the river
and the door opens. It is the air. It is invisible
Elijah walking in.

Memory, Summer

Summer. In its mornings were calls of swifts and swallows
wheeling and circling, as if marking out whirlwinds,

and, in its evenings, unfailing wails of cicadas, fading then
mounting then fading, deeper in moth-haunted night.

In its passings, each cloud was a many decked ship, and there
were a good many of them,

and, under its shinings, each leaf turned into a basking butterfly,
of which there was an inexhaustible if intermittent supply.

On its winds blew scented memories and premonitions of
worlds engraved into the farther side of the word *beyond*, as
on flipsides of unminted coins,

And, on its stillnesses, you could examine a single fern frond and
see its spore-laden surface, magnified in intricate detail, like
the citadel of a beehive on the verge of swarming.

Against its sturdy weight, you could poise a recumbent glance
and experience waking as a geometrically expanding process

until the speed of events accelerated so far past your ability to
register them that presence merged with oblivion,

or else geared down to the indolent seepage, the luxurious ooz-
ing, of oil.

Time also did many things at once, for example, flattening into
the unbearably hallucinatory undulations of sand dunes,

which would never bear the mirage of an oasis, stunning you
with purposelessness, with vacancy,

yet simultaneously bearing so relentlessly down upon you, from
such unbearable heights, so vertically, so vertiginously,

as to induce unremitting head-splitting dizziness, even though
down its headlong shaft you could tumble unendingly

like a diving seabird into many bannered unpartitioned child-
hood, yet never break its meniscus, never grasp the silver
treasures darting, drifting, swirling there,

while from its silence you could compose a percussive sym-
phony and, on that silence print it perfectly, thanks to

drumbeats of beetles' wings camouflaging themselves in fur-
rows of tree bark, gurglings of sap in trees' veins,

drip-drip of galaxies echoing in petalled bowls of flowers and
clack of grasshoppers landing safe on miracles,

hiss of dews evaporating from grass blades and whooshings of
burning-out shooting stars,

churnings, crunchings and clatterings of fine-grained blinks of
sand swept up in crests of breaking adorations,

unrolling, by way of one interruption interrupting another,
interruption overlaying interruption, multiple layerings,

falls and rapids, symphonies and cacophonies, longings and belongings, currents and torrents, of interruptions –

Summer: yes, you could drink it to its uttermost dregs, knowing, so long as consciousness held, this was incorruptible.

Silken thread: gypsy's song

Here is a song to be played and sung by a gypsy
tumbling and soaring from his accordion
and his fellow's on a violin. Mist and rain
were among the ancestors of this melody
but there is nothing blurred or uncertain about it.
It is a silken thread. The light strikes it many ways,
like a knife honed sharp, but its stab withheld.

Silken thread: poet's pages

And here is a written page, with no crossings out,
in swift Cyrillic on a table on a balcony,
corners fluttering in breeze, held down by a coin
from the pocket of the man who wrote the script
which dearly the wind would have loved
to snatch away. The man, who went inside to talk
on the telephone to someone from abroad,
has never returned to the balcony.

The face of light

There is a face that appears on a ray of light
and it has a precise and unforgettable expression,
and if one were not to behave entirely as a stranger
and if one were to be honest and cast away prejudice
and if one were to grant it the justice it deserves,
one would have to admit and recognise that this smile,
which is not exactly a smile, but a kind of self-settlement
in absorbed repose, and one of the conditions of beauty,
belongs to a white angel, with darkening, blue tipped wings.

All you need to be is a competent, not perfect, receiver.
All you need to ask for is the partial but authentic
truthfulness of a witness, who cannot see or hear everything
or even be expected to. Allowances are made
for sincerity, and even good intentions.
All you need to do is remember that you are part
of this light, in it and of it, as guest is to host,
and that you belong to it, even though the light itself
is wholly merciless, and eventually will devour you.

The voice of light

Listen. There is also a voice, riverborne or seaborne,
but always close to water. I have heard it along the Danube
as I walked – on the midnight of my forty sixth birthday
remembering my father – from Zemun to the Ušče
where the Sava joins the Danube, and faces Kalemegdan.
and there, above, was my nightingale, pouring out his heart
in improbable celebration, a heavenly companion
suddenly, unexpectedly, commentating, rephrasing
summer peace in the soul and harmony of the world.

Harvest

Again I turn the key and the house I knew
is different. Where once were only walls
hung with paintings and shadows, now
through the room there's a door
which I approach and open. Corridors
give on corridors, airier, higher ceilinged
than any remembered spaces that called
from here before. French windows
open on a patio paved in dappled slabs.
A vine drips mellow clusters in sheens
of mist and cloud. Beneath it, a bow-leggèd table
and chairs in matching wrought iron
rest half in sunlight, half under greeny shade.
On the table, bread, peppers, olives,
cheese, salt and white wine. All this is waiting
for you, and perhaps me too. But certainly
to me, this bird-filled, herb-scented garden
sloping behind it as far as the reedy river
with that familiar tangy offshore breeze
wafting in from the estuary, and that outline
of mountains, like boats adrift on haze, is
more enticing than harvests of childhood.

The man I met on the hill

The man I met on the hill was looking the other way.
But he was the one I followed. I called him *Rabbi* and *Master*
which only made him laugh. Look at your boots, he said
without so much as a glance. Make sure your laces are tied.

5 On the death of Ivan V. Lalić

Nobody dies too late, O lords of the far side
Of curiosity, nobody ever dies too late
To find an open door. Someone will be waiting to wipe
The blood from his frightened lip, to name
Him once and for all.

IVAN V. LALIĆ

You cannot find me any image for
Our knowledge of our ignorance of the dead.

JAMES BURNS SINGER

This door I can't unlatch

You have boomeranged time back
to its cluster of origins. You have unsewn
the garment this moment is and unreeled
the spindle of action back into first desire.

What would happen, I ask, *if I were to call*
your name? I do so. Nothing shrinks.
No harm seems to be done.
Nothing disappears. Nothing else dies.

Your photographs in my head are ikons
that won't stop moving. The mirror behind
me shows you this side of the wall
in a white corner. But the cold fact is

there's no breath in the adjacent room
you are in on the other side of this
door I can't unlatch wherever I am or these
words more than lap and erode like tides.

What did you mean by it?

What did you mean by it, Ivan, going off alone
so sudden and so soon, abandoning us to
join the ever-swelling armies of the unseeable
unswayable dead, you we had counted on
    to stay among us, defend us? Now
      wherever we look for you, gaps appear –
gaps never noticed that had always been there,
gaps new-formed and forming, gaps between gaps,
at our table, in our minds, gaps in space itself. Almost
as if residual emptiness were being forced to make
uneasy confession that you had betrayed us by joining
those we most fear for ever. So now should we call up
professional mourners with gnarled wringing hands
emptied and let them wail, or listen to the inevitable
clacketing of pipes under bare wooden floorboards
suddenly gone cold? You I vainly address here with no
address, we who remember you, walk streets and lanes
in your absence, and for me even after all these years
there is no respite. I look for you to talk to and
    pass back answers you uniquely
    could confer, sudden, simple and
    dazzling as a torch flare in a cave
or shooting star in a cloudless mid-August
the night of harvest princesses. That light breeze
your speech is gone for good and what little I achieve
here of my silly aims without you to consult
is ineffectual air. Oh yes I suppose irreversible
time and the world will fill up the gap you are
again with colours, movements, longings, and
I move on and gloze over them. Death swelled
in you like a sap and blossomed and fruited through
you and swallowed you back into its black hole.

One day you wake up

Then one day you wake
up and the corridor is
closed, the daily one you use
always, to everywhere. You scrabble
for your keys amid the clutter. Still
you are able to do things and have not lost
all mobility. But you find the one key
that does not fit anyway and suspect
isn't even yours. You hear the tearing
of paper, muttering of muffled voices
and, somewhere near, the clattering of heels.

On the street outside your window
a young woman, unknown,
is walking away from you,
on her way to work.
Now you remember and too late recognise,
all your life this morning and every other
morning, this same young woman
has always been walking away from you,
and each of those previous repetitions has been
a slightly discomfiting, even irritating forewarning,
an altogether anxiety-provoking rehearsal
for this. And now the moment itself
has arrived in full process and will no doubt
reach finality, it all seems perfectly ordinary,
even banal. In this double frame
of event and expectation,
of time interior and time exterior,
the copy precedes the original.

Always she has been walking away from you
disappearing around the next corner before
you could entertain even the chance of catching
the merest sideview of the contours of her face

in the sharp angle of shadow, falling almost
horizontally, from the indented light of morning
except in last remnants of dissolving dreams
which this light has failed to devour and you
have not forgotten quite entirely enough
not to recognise. Whatever season it is
this limpid light has the tarnished sheen,
dented and fingerprinted, of long unpolished
silver and texture of very light chain mail.

    Whatever will be taken away
    must be released without
    question. Whatever will
    dissolve cannot be clung to. All
expectations will be reft from you for ever.
Whether you catch a glimpse of her face or not,
relish this bitter light when all the rehearsals stop.

Are you there?

Are you there? Who reads this I know
will not be you really. Not ever. The anyone
who may respond to the open call this is – by
picking this up – arrives or will arrive later, while
you are and were coterminous and before. I say
coterminous because the you who in particular
I address now, dead man, as though you were alive
is you and only you. And anyone else, that is, every
one who arrives here and may hear this, overhears
a mere kind-of-private conversation. They may
say or think *monologue* but how do they know
anything of the provenance of these words
most of which are yours not mine. And I say *before*
because the way you were – I mean your particular
mode of being *you* – spoke always as if from forever
in my head – just as you are now really. And even
now the many ways I see you are far more clear
than definite as you move, talk, peer, poke around
in my mind. I almost believe I could summon you
at will and I may well do so. But the telephone
keeps barking from another world where no-one
is ready, willing or available even to say Hello
and when I stumble across the floor to grab it,
even before my answering machine kicks in
with its neutered voice that isn't even mine,
the line goes dead. I dial callback to find
no-one and no reference. Whoever the caller was
     chose not to leave a number. But I know
     it was you, don't I? And nobody fools me.

Deliberate, slow, meditative as in an old movie,
     I place the receiver on the desk and it
rings again and, still from the other room
behind the door I've now closed against it,
goes on ringing like a small yellow mountainous

wild flower I do not know how to name, crannied
in a rock against the wind. Dead friend,
although no doubt from time to time memory
will play more tricks by calling herself you, and
although your works live, I fear your time is no
longer now any more and will never come again.

Even when you lived

Even when you lived, your carved poems wore
the dead's petrified garments. They fitted you well
in this world. Scarves of limestone karst, moulded
from dolomite pillars, marble handkerchiefs sliced
out of walls of caves, necklaces of pebbles fingered

from the Rovinj seabed, black snows of darkness
melted by a candle flame, needles and lances of ice
hoisted from the underworld: these vestments
and ornaments your poems calmly bore, draped
on their stony forms, creases ironed in time.

And, carved out of their cores, monumental voices
called from zones abandoned, in scarce-recorded
tongues, Thracian, Dacian, Decian, Illyrian,
Etruscan: *Phersipnai Prsepna Phersipnei*. And
Orpheus himself came sauntering out of Rhodope.

Here a god, a heroine, a mother of gods, a saint,
there a guard, a gardener, a beekeeper, a mariner,
and among them, radiant-eyed, robed in white and
blue, ringed edges shimmering, in suns, stars, fires,
your sturdiest protectors, twice-born Balkan angels.

And, darker still, more furtive, glimpsed far beneath,
secréted from deepest shadows, anterior to shadow,
blind maddened sirens, urchins, monstrous sea-imps,
rockfaced giants, gargoyles and goblins of caverns
drooled, howled, roared, crooned, complained.

Nobody dies too late

Nobody dies too late, you said, ever to be admitted,
to find the right officials and appropriate ministers.
The lords of the far side are hospitable, welcoming,
their door stands always open, no-one is turned away,
they'll send someone to meet you whenever you arrive.

Nobody ever fails to receive the compassion denied
supplicants and beggars this side of the one-way
frontier, arms outstretched, needy and wrétchèd,
hands scrabbling and pleading, fingers bleeding,
crushed against the barrier, barely breathing air.

Nobody dies too late? But you died too early. Your
unwritten and half-written poems should have
slithered through Death's nets, cheated Him of His
catch, swum back here where they belong, with us,
not be left to cluster, piled high among Immortals.

What waste, the flesh and entrails of your poems
delivered to those gluttons to devour. What difference
would it have made to them, copiously supplied
with never-ending feasts of the richest variety,
to have been kept waiting for you a little longer?

You departed too early and arrived unexpected.
What mantle did you assume and to what rank rise
to abandon us so suddenly? How jealous I am,
dead man, that they who need no nourishment
should deprive us, deprive *me*, of your company.

Lords of the far side

Lords of the far side. How formally
you addressed them. But it isn't their plural
hordes, interminable multitudes, or even select
representatives I call for, call to, call on here,
but you, my close, loved, unique friend.

Often, when living, did you address the far
dead as I do you here. Were your speeches then
meant as recommendations on etiquette for
approaching *you*, once you too had gone over?
Commander? Marshall? Minister? Chancellor?

When you were alive, we crossed gulfs
on the familiar bridge of the second
person singular. Made to sway, flex, bend,
it stretched across silences, on suspensions
finely poised, and never gave way beneath us.

Precision-bombed by order of Commodore
Death, that bridge is in smithereens
and not to be rebuilt by engineer, doctor
or priest. Old friend, now you're accessible
only through hints, half-tints, murmurings,

echoes, shadows and, most oblique of all, symbols,
if I'm to track you across and through them,
must I follow the precedent of your own
standing protocols by distantly, courteously,
cordially, addressing you too now as *My Lord*?

The unready ones

Like bridges patrolled by reticent sentinels
ordered to screen all arrivals

                          your poems
demarcate the precise frontiers between
        the shore you've gone over to
        and us, the unready ones

            Try to steal across
        snatch an instant's echo
the bridge suspensions rattle
                          gates
            come clanging down
                    and all around sirens
                        wail like starving wolves

        Invariably we fail
                until once   for all time
        we too are dragged across
            by icy fingered guardians

we who are always
            flawed
    easy to break as worm-gnawed planks
        imperfectly tuned
                as poorly sealed drums

Not the dead but Death

Not the dead but Death,
not the dead but their Master
    Invisible, Invincible,
All-Powerful, took you.

I can't imagine the Overlord
of those realms welcoming you,
    wiping tears from your eyes.
Or mine. Or anyone else's.

Randomly merciless
and selectively cruel, is
    how I envisage
Him. Relishing atrocity.

Life spins gift and miracle.
Death exacts final payment
    The effort costs
Him absolutely nothing.

Nothing, hollow ring

Invisible Master, greediest
and richest plutocrat, You
    who remove everything,
    stockpile it for Yourself,
what do You give in return?

Nothing: key to Your character,
scope, behaviour, deeds.
    Nothing, hollow ring bound
    and binding to darkness
no end or way out.

Nothing, void's warp and woof
that begins wherewhen end
    harmonies plucked on strings
    of matter and energy.
Nothing, Your fine protection

of every human destiny.
Nothing, whitened blur of
    wolves howling across
    snow dyke and dune
as time for numbing comes.

Nothing, placeless, wordless
dissolution of identity
    You have cast
    and clouded over
my friend, the poet Lalić.

One iota of respect?

Now I can't see you, except in my own head,
can't hear you, except through your poems,
can't catch your drift, except among
stony images, why should I entertain
one iota of respect for those unassailable

giants who have robbed you from us,
assimilated you among them, granted you
their citizenship and a passport that allows
you to flit unaccompanied, at your will or theirs,
or, perhaps, only at *their* arbitrary calling

back and forth through time, when here
among us, for the living, was where
you were needed? To reach the guarded
gate inset in the wall that enshrines
your sacred inner office, shall I be kept

shuffling in a queue of muttering supplicants
before gaining admittance to your secret
chancery? Where should I queue, Lord Ivan?
In the echoing roofed stadium? At the barrier
to the platform of King's Cross Station? Or in

the beige walled corridor of the old asylum?
Now that all your faces have faded and gone
invisible, will your cool assistant nurse boom
my name through her microphone or bleep it
in red corpuscles on her moving black screen?

Tissue of waterfalls

At the border of the finite world
a semi-permeable membrane
has sieved you away from us,
      web of intangible skin
meshed of one-way valves.

From the cliff, indiscernible,
of each sharpened instant,
at the root tip and twig end
      of every quantum of distance,
your substance, being of finest

most delicate texture, has now
been poured out, has vanished
even from scattered smoke.
      Nor do you reside in dust.
Or ash. Or powder. But if the soul

like the body is seven tenths water
must that part, if only that, not
be present everywhere? Tissue of
      waterfalls, river mist, sea spray,
nets of nested morning, haze veiling

valley folds and faces of fields,
what apologies you do deign, drain
expectation, muffle and blur hope
      and soak away, as I come
among you, calling my friend Lalić.

From the other shore

From the other shore
      the dead
   maintain proper distance
         their faces fade
   unapproachable

except in dreams and poems

But for your poems, would you
not have dissolved
     entirely
in mist and cloud?

When I hear you now, you who were once
         my friend
   have become as vague and general
as the wind about this rented house
     half a mile from the sea

You boom and rustle at me, you
   whirl strange things around
and I hear, or think I hear,
   from the next room, your voice

I strain again, hear nothing, breathe
     twice and listen

     Nothing, an irretrievable
     distance between us

  except in poems and dreams

Here at Ballyhealy
  on the other edge of Europe

      again I walk out and again

          trample the same empty
  nine mile stretch of sand

Aristocrats of silence

Poets never belong wholly to this world. They
catch echoes, snatch murmurs, hardly understood,
on breezes from the dead lands. From the dead
they take authority as imperfect interpreters. When
poets speak, the dead lean on their shoulders.

Prematurely the Immortals made you their trusted
messenger. Too much, to be such a vessel
without winged helmet or sandals, without even
a mediating angel's sturdy staff. The Immortals
blew through you as if you were their reed.

That thrumming outside? That was not the wind.
on Kosmaj. That chatter was not of rain
prattling at the window. That was the dead,
tugging at your wrists, whispering in your ear,
distilling in you your poems of liquid flame.

And when you joined those aristocrats of silence,
I dreamed we'd sealed up your eyes and ears,
your mouth and nostrils, with beeswax. As if
you had been perfected. As if you had been sculpted
into a marble monument. Pedestalled and tableted.

Not so, you drum on the other side of the air
tunnelled into my thorax. *Not so*, you brush on
cymbals of my sleeping eyelids. *Never*, you write
on the flight of a blue butterfly that settles
on my left forefinger. *Not while the living live.*

Dictated by a man who is dead

You do keep coming back. Where you have descended
Ivan, cantor of Balkan light, can't be buried so
terribly deep in silence's citadel. You can't be
lost for good in the all-penetrating darkness
permanently lurking in every shadow's heartland.

You do keep coming back. You glance through
my winter window and cover my hands
on the keyboard. *This* letter, *not* that.
You ride on crests of words and at words'
intersections with silences spread a kind of haze,

rings of colours meshing between its wavering
borders, shot through with brilliances, that
refract edges and platforms shared among
witless things. On a velvet August night when
meteorites are showering, you come back

to the villages, into the fields and woods
between desire and perfection and to those
looking out to sea and scanning the horizon
for islands. You flicker against walls
in shadows scattered by the candles

from Friday evening's table. To children
around bonfires, what I hear you saying is
The book is perfect but can never be completed.
This was dictated by a man who is dead.
The book is always survivor.

Backgrounded among these

From profiles of medicinal shrubs, stomata
of ferns and mosses, wrinklings and stretchings
of time in those quieter places such as hollows
of hills where wind talks and sometimes sings
among rocks, very high up on mountains and

down caves haunted by back-flying butterflies,
and where water flows, fluent in gushing springs,
babbling and burbling in rivulets and cursing
and screaming down rapids – there is your voice,
brother. And there in an eyeblink, *your face.*

The bowl of light fills and empties

You conducted precision surgeries in the bodies
of superstitions. You mended images' bones. You
hammered sparks in silences. Then a sudden

fissure in the surface of normal time, a glitch
in the day's fabric. You forfeited your place
on this side. Children, more and more of them,

occupy it, babbling. They keep coming forward, with
eager open faces, arriving from apparent nothing.
Between that glory and this, full of blissful forgettings,

they have not been taught to remember. Time
will start happening again once they have
been taught. Who shall understand the miracle

of these gatherings, arrivals, dispersals? The bowl
of light fills and empties, empties and refills.

6 Things in their miracles

. . . consciousness results from superradiance, a rippling cascade
of subatomic particles – when individual quantum particles
such as photons lose their individuality and begin acting as a
single unit . . .

LYNNE MCTAGGART

In some beliefs, the pointing (index) finger is [. . .] the finger of
life, while the middle finger is the finger of death. In another
belief, the pointing finger is that of the Lord of Words, while
the middle finger is the finger of the word itself. In [this]
context, the pointing finger embeds both symbolisms: the
finger of life is the finger of the word itself, that is, of the poem
itself.

SLOBODAN RAKITIĆ

Pure blue, and cool

The first touch past tragedy is miracle and
an improbable unexpected roaring. Reality
gashes wide. Through this gap pours more
than memory accounted for or ever could.
Things open mouths and speak. Everything
does just and precisely that, without exception,
without squeak or drawing the slightest attention
to itself as solipsist or soloist above any other
competing component. Their unique voices
are now and clear, all of them. What they say
is not uttered or utterable in echoes, hints,
indecipherable murmurings, comparisons and
still less, symbols and images. Especially not
symbols and images. What they say is what
they do and are, not expression or outcome
of what they would be. Or 'feel like'. Or 'know'.
What happens is *this*. The multiple preciousness
of everything, every thing – in its thingness, its
thinghood – leaves no space, place, grace even
for emotion. Emotions might well track back
later in mirror-play. This is pure blue, and cool.

For what it is

The second touch is received only for what
it is and what you are. It is accepted as a fine
and necessary but by no means extraordinary
or special part of things in their miracles.

Things in their miracles

The pity is words that come later
in their honest attempts to truth-tell
by falling into symbols cannot fail
to lie. Things in their miracles
are radiant with eternities
at every blink of momenthood.
Their revolvings into contraries
and turnings into elsenesses
are themselves their speech.

Unseeable gate through air

Blue creature, this poem,
at all times and places
you open an unseeable
gate through air and
by doing so you
write yourself and dissolve
all stretches and passages
of 'linear' time 'between'
and 'contained in' and
'precisely demarcated by'
the two-way flow, spread,
thrust, thread, trust, etc.
of mutual recognition in
and of the persons adopted
by our unique and singular
I and you, through this.

Finger of life, finger of the word

Here is the finger of life, finger of the word.
Pointing at whom? At what?

                           At you. And the earth
you live on. And, of course, at the sky. As if with
a mind of its own, the hand the finger belongs to
rotates, palm upwards. A question is being offered.
A request is being made.

7 The Apple

Recalling Šumarice

As you touched me, blue butterfly,
there was a kind of mingling. You reached
     towards me and grew in me.
You took me and became me. A slow stain
     spread through me, that will not
disappear. *Down, to* and *through* a self
     no longer mine or own, in silent
speech I said, 'Fly back and tell them,
     wherever, whoever, your
lords, masters, mistresses – from
     now on and ever I am registered
yours and theirs: approved page,
     vassal, apprentice, aspiring
contracted novice.' The fatal graze
     and brush of your almost
weightless weight has closed in
     me a compact doubly more
durable than brotherhood by blade.
     No voice before or since has
wounded so irrevocably or called
     such hospitality. What
indiscernible wingflick, on scent
     track or wind change
crabbed your flight at my angle,
     you minister of quietness,
Hermes to underworlds, gift-bearing
     clarion, harbinger and blue
herald? No more would the scales
     tip, that balance light and
dark, were an angel to fall and
     pin me to a stone. You
swelled through and overran me.
     What ever I was is gone.

What is Destiny, then, but what
    you make and follow? You've
blessed, not with visible sign, but
    sightless inner counterbond,
guardian and living talisman against
    being fooled by bondages.
Not with a birthmark. A deathmark.

When Death's door was locked

When Death's door was locked
from my conscious awareness
    and I could not see in,
though in bone, nerve and skin
    aware of its nearness,
all my talents lay blocked
as behind a huge boulder
    deep in a cave.
Now, as I grow older
and nearer the grave
    the lid on the latch
opens up eye and soul
and helps me detach
    flesh from my goal.
As fires blaze reflected
    in glistening metals,
that light, resurrected
in poems and songs,
    falls like rose petals –
and the stone rolls away
and how my gift flows
and flowers like a rose
    in relinquishing day.

Topčider, October

This slanting light through branches
quivers on burning leaves. Balkan light
again. But this time, *no dead*. These
voices don't belong to them
and don't bear their wounds.

From everywhere and nowhere
they call. And they'll keep calling.
Now even their echoes
belong to their own presences
not to detached ghosts.

Snagging on trunks and branches,
chill wind hums. Each thing
overpours its boundedness
in bounty, plenty, plenitude.
This spilling onto the day is

all this light is and betokens.
Its meaning is what it is.
Trammelled into the stuff of things
finest meshes and filters
channel braided glories

each with unique voice. Treetops
flare and flurry, ringed
in translucent radiance.
Rare the grasp or hold but ever
the glimpse, graze, touch.

The apple

The last thing he dreamed about
was digging a small hole
half a metre across, one metre deep

and layering it with loam
in the quiet walled courtyard
seven paces from the back door

of his own familiar house
that, outside the dream, he knew
wasn't his at all

at the edge of the village in Serbia
which, in the dream, was his home
although outside sleep and death

he had never lived there, never
would – and on the loam placing
a large sturdy rounded pink apple,

covering topsoil over it, packing
it lightly down, and prodding
a stake in, to mark its position.

Woman reading

With the light pinned to your chest
    like a medal
you sit at the window
      in the slanting shaft
        of afternoon.

Faith

Out of spaces deeper
than dreamed by sleeper
and towards zones higher
than imaged through desire
the poem puts out threads
and climbs and spreads.

RB
BELGRADE, ZEMUN, SPLIT,
TENERIFE, TEPLICE, TUSCANY, BERLIN,
BALLYHEALY AND CAMBRIDGE
1985–2007

Postscript and Notes

Postscript

This book consists of poems 'set' in former Yugoslavia. Following half a dozen visits to Serbia, Croatia and Slovenia between 1982 and 1986, I lived in Belgrade from 1987 to 1991. During this time, my work and interests took me to all the Yugoslav republics: Slovenia, Croatia, Bosnia & Hercegovina, Macedonia, Montenegro and Serbia, as well as to the autonomous provinces of Kosovo and Vojvodina. In this book I have set out to explore the particular slants and angles on life that, in my perception and understanding, are Balkan. These aren't easy to characterise. If there is a key, a password, I think it might be *epiphany* – though not conceived of as a rare event, privileged experience, special bonus, or even as a sort of stretchmark in time, but rather as a shared ingredient of the day-to-day, a common component in the condition and conduit of consciousness, wavephase in the continuum of being.

But waves have their troughs as well as peaks. Coinciding with the years I lived there, before my eyes and under my feet, Yugoslavia began to implode. These were low times in the Balkans. Yawning deep and disastrous, troughs turned into nadirs. Within a few years, around and during this time, many good friends of mine died, including some of the country's best writers.

While *epiphany* suggests bounty, an overspilling of harmonies into radiant clarity, the word *Balkan* itself implies the diametrical opposite. *Balkanisation*: fragmentation, division, dispersal, dissolution.

At the time of writing this, the Balkans have been rebalkanised. All six Yugoslav republics have been turned into independent countries. But whatever new divisions and separations the border-makers may draw up, whatever alliances and realignments merge and emerge, and regardless of the shifting patterns between centrifugal and centripetal pulls, I do think that there are modes of seeing, experiencing and being-in-the-world that are recognizably Balkan, in that they belong communally and durably to all the diverse parts of this complicated and fragmented geo-cultural zone.

This view was also held by the Yugoslav and Mediterranean poet Ivan V. Lalić.[1] The dedication of this book to his memory arises mainly out of a desire to offer a homage and a testament. I mean this as one friend to another, one poet to another. To me Ivan was a kind of wise and knowledgeable older brother. In our conversations, ideas triggered fast, and we often thought of the same things at the same time and finished each other's sentences. I learned an enormous amount from him. His poems have not only called me. They have resonated for me as tuning instruments for my own. But the dedication to him has been chosen and placed in this book for another reason too: I think Ivan Lalić's poetry epitomises the Balkan way of being, perceiving and experiencing.[2]

Every *topos* that invites being lived in – and lived through – deserves respect, understanding, discernment, honour and love. The real zone that these poems draw on, and are drawn from, is a resilient and complex one, deep and echoic in scope as well as broad and varied in span. Clearly, all such zones defy any poetic response that is either akin to occupation or aligned with appropriation, and still more, they rightly repel the entire possible gamut of 'treatments' that either of such sad approaches inevitably drags in its wake.

With respect to the topography of the particular place-in-a-time and time-in-a-place that went by the name *Yugoslavia*, as well as to Yugoslavia's successors, these are challenges that have been presented and present to me, under Balkan light. I have done my best to accept, grasp and fulfil them. I take responsibility, of course, for all gaps, shortcomings and distortions arising out of my own biases, blindspots and errors in placement, focus, holding and attentiveness.

RB
CAMBRIDGE
AUGUST 2, 2008

---

[1] See Lalić's essay, 'Some Notes on Yugoslav Literature: a Historical Approach', in *Out of Yugoslavia*, guest-edited by Richard Burns and Stephen Markovich, North Dakota Quarterly, 61/1, Winter 1993, pp. 12–17.

[2] In the various prefaces and introductions to his four books of translations of Ivan V. Lalić's poems, Francis R. Jones explores and clarifies some of these complexities, overlays and nexuses and explains convincingly how and why Lalić was both a Yugoslav and a Mediterranean poet. See: *The Works of Love, Last Quarter, The Passionate Measure* and *A Rusty Needle* (Anvil Press Poetry, London, respectively 1981, 1987, 1989 and 1996).

Notes

shows part of the fresco of the *Angel at Christ's Tomb* in Mileševa Monastery, usually known as *The White Angel*, a masterpiece of Serbian medieval art. Mileševa was founded by King Vladislav in the 13th century. See also POEM FOR MY INFANT DAUGHTER AT MILEŠEVA MONASTERY, pp. 52–55, ON THE QUALITIES OF LIGHT IN THE BALKANS, pp. 34–35, THE FACE OF LIGHT, p. 92, and the notes to these poems on pp. 150, 153 and 157.

DO VIDJENA DANITSÉ, (Goodbye Balkan Belle), pp. 1–15

'Danitsé': transliteration of the vocative form of the Serbian *Danice*; nominative, *Danica*: a woman's name, and the morning star. The accent placed on the last syllable indicates that the final 'e' is pronounced.

Written in Cambridge: between November 1997 and July 2007.

p. 1, Epigraph: *Uvek si mi draga bila / Domovino moja mila*: ['Always you have always been dear to me / My kind homeland']. Part of the chorus of a once popular patriotic song that celebrated the territories and landscapes of former Yugoslavia and their variety. I heard it in Arandjelovac in 1982, a few days after first arriving in Yugoslavia. The next lines give more clues: *Od Vardara pa do Triglava / Od Djerdapa pa do Jadrana* ['From the Vardar to Triglav / From Djerdap to the Adriatic']. The Vardar is in the extreme south of former Yugoslavia (Greek Axiós), a river that rises in Macedonia and flows into the Aegean in the Gulf of Salonika. *Triglav* marks the north, the highest peak in Slovenia. *Djerdap* is in North East Serbia, where there is a gorge and a hydroelectric station across the Danube, near the Romanian border.

p. 3, *Voždovac*, district of Belgrade, on a hill.

p. 3, *rakija*, raki, alcoholic spirit.

p. 3, *Zlatibor* ['Golden pine'], mountain in western Serbia, 230 km from Belgrade; holiday area, where many *vikendice* ['weekend chalets'] have been built.

p. 3, *Mrčajevci*, village in *Šumadija* ['Woodland'], central Serbia.

p. 3, *Smederevo*, Serbian town whose large medieval fort, built in 1430, overlooks the Danube. See also pp. 33 and 34.

p. 3, *Zadar, Trogir, Omiš, Šibenik*, towns on the Dalmatian coast, Croatia.

p. 3, *Brač, Hvar*, Dalmatian islands close to the Croatian mainland.

p. 4, *Ragusa*, medieval name for Dubrovnik and for the maritime republic based in that city, which rivalled Venice. Ragusa grew powerful between the 14th and 17th centuries and became a centre for literature and the arts.

p. 4, *Salonae*, later *Salona, Salon*, and now *Solin*, a suburb of *Split*: large ancient Dalmatian coastal city and partially Hellenised fortress of the tribe of the Delmatae; later conquered by the Romans and capital of the Roman province of Dalmatia.

p. 4, *Senj*, Dalmatian port ruled by pirates. See the next note.

p. 4, 'Uskoks' [lit. 'pouncers, jumpers']: pirates of the Adriatic. In *The Uskoks of Senj: Piracy, Banditry, and Holy War in the Sixteenth-Century Adriatic* (Cornell University Press, Ithaca, 1992), Catherine Wendy Bracewell explores their history, their multi-ethnic composition, their social and military codes and their lifestyle in fascinating and brilliant detail. Almost half a century earlier, in the course of a description of her visit to Senj, Rebecca West devoted five pages of scintillating writing to their history, explaining how the Uskoks had fled west from the invading Turks sweeping northwards through Bulgaria, Serbia and Bosnia; how they transformed themselves into a highly organised naval power, first controlling the narrow straight between Senj and the long, narrow island of Krk; how they then 'chased the Turkish ships up and down the Adriatic, stripped them, and sank them'; how 'for nearly thirty years they lived in such a state of legitimate and disciplined warfare that they attacked only Turkish ships'; and how, following their sense of betrayal after the Venetian-Turkish deal in the 1530's, from 1566 on they 'became gangsters of the sea.' (Rebecca West, *Black Lamb and Grey Falcon*, Macmillan, London, 1977 edition, pp. 124–128.)

p. 4, 'Vlachs' (also known as Aromanians and Tzantzariia): a transhument Balkan people of uncertain origins, whose language, heavily influenced by Latin, belongs to the 'Eastern Romance' group. The words *Vlach, Wallachian* (Greek *Vlachos*, Serbian & Croatian *vlah*, pl. *vlasi*, etc.), which belong to a set widely distributed through most Germanic languages, are cognate with names attributed to many different ethnic and tribal groupings. The meaning of the Germanic term is 'foreigner'. Compare for example Eng. *Welsh*, Fr. *Wallon*, Fr. *Gaule*, Eng. *Gaul*.

In the Balkans, including Greece, the epithet 'Vlach' was and in some regions still is used as a pejorative term for an individual or member of a group, usually not one's own, whom a speaker might consider inferior, less cultured, less civilised, etc. In former Yugoslavia, it referred specifically to Serbs, with very strong pejorative overtones. In an essay about rainmaking customs in the regions of Kordun, Banija and Moslavina, Dražen Nožinić writes:

> The most widespread group within the three examined regions were Serbs of the Orthodox religion. All surrounding Croats (and Muslims) used to call those Serbs *Vlasi* (*Vlahi* or *Vlaji* – i.e. Vlachs). According to my tellers, the rural Serbs used those names themselves till World War II, though, after 1945, the term *Serbs* become widely accepted and established. Many of them also said they considered the term 'Vlach' offensive. According to the area, there were also other names for Serbs and all of them were considered offensive and disparaging [. . .] The only name noted in Moslavina for Serbs was 'Vlach'. One particular group among the Serbs are those in Žumberk belonging to the Greek-Catholic religion who call themselves *Uskoci*, while the surrounding Slovenians and Croats call them *Vlasi*.

(*Raskovnik*, No. 91–92, Belgrade, 1998. pp. 77 ff. *tr. Vera V. Radojević & RB*.)

In 1630, the Hapsburg emperor proclaimed the so-called *Statuta Wallachorum* ['Vlach Statute'], which regulated the status of the so-called Vlach settlers, who in fact also comprised Serbs, Croats and others. These were emigrants, refugees and displaced persons who had escaped from the Ottoman Empire. The document defined their military command, their obligations and rights to internal self-administration. These people settled as guards, protectors and patrollers of the frontiers against the Turks, for example in the *Krajina* in Croatia. This was the border-region between Christian and Islamic dominated regions. See also the note on *Krajina*, p. 147 below.

p. 4, 'Morlachs'. Variant term for 'Vlach', used along the Dalmatian coast (Croatian *Morlak*, pl. *Morovlah*, *Morlaci*, and Italian *Morlacco*, pl. *Morlacchi*). According to the *Oxford English Dictionary* (OED online version, 2006), the term originates in Byzantine Greek, combining the roots *mavros* ['black'] and *vlachos* ['Vlach']. This passed into 12th century Latin as *Morovlachus*, with variants *Moroblachus*, *Morolacchus*, and from 1420, *Morlachus*, *Morlacchus* and the corruption *Nigri Latini* ['Black Latins']. The OED also suggests that the 'Black Vlachs' were so named because of the colour of their clothes, and adds: 'A member of a Vlach people centred originally on the eastern Adriatic port of Ragusa (modern Dubrovnik), and later inhabiting more northerly parts of the Dalmatian coast and its hinterland, the whole region being known at one time as Morlacchia.'

p. 4, *Kaštel Stari* ['Old Castle'], village north of Split.

p. 4, *Sinj*, small town in the hills behind Split where each August a festival called the *Alka* takes place to commemorate the defeat of the Turks in 1715. This event involves a parade of local men dressed up in medieval costumes, followed by a tournament in which lance-bearing horseback-riders attempt to pierce a suspended metal ring, which is called the *alka*, while galloping at high speed along a single list.

p. 4, *joyeuse-triste jolie-laide*, French oxymorons: 'happy-sad, ugly-pretty'.

p. 4, *Sarajevo*, capital of Bosnia.

p. 4, *Kalemegdan*, huge rambling fortress and open space in Belgrade, overlooking the confluence of the Rivers Danube and Sava. One of the great parks of Europe.

p. 5, *Bežanija*, area in New Belgrade on the northern bank of the River Sava, developed after the Second World War and characterised by row on row of modernist apartment blocks.

p. 5, *Ušće*, 'estuary': northern riverbank park-area of Belgrade facing the fortress of Kalemegdan, where the Sava flows into the Danube.

p. 5, 'Hotel International, Hotel Global, Hotel Startime, Hotel Galactic': the hotel names are fictitious but in combination with 'mobster bosses [. . .] biggest /and ugliest of the big-time thugs', the implicit reference is to Hotel Jugoslavija in Zemun, where Željko Ražnatović *aka* Arkan was gunned down on January 5, 2000. Arkan was at various times a small-time criminal, an international government-paid assassin, a gangster boss, a gun-runner, leader of the paramilitary group known as 'The Tigers' and a Serbian nationalist politician.

p. 5, *Smederevo*: see the note on p. 141 above.

p. 5, *Petrovaradin*: castle on the Danube facing Novi Sad, capital of Vojvodina. The name figures in a famous 'Old Town Song', *Osam tamburaša* ['Eight tamburaša' – stringed instruments, like small lutes].

p. 5, Approximate translations of titles of Old Town Songs: *Stop Flowing River* ['Zaustavite Dunav']; *It Ain't Worth Crying* ['Ne vredi plakati']; *My Sweet Little Marijana* ['Slatka moja Marijana', a Dalmatian love song]; *I've Just One Wish* ['Imam jednu želju']; *My Man Milan* ['Moj Milane'] and *Days When I Don't Know What I'll Do* ['Ima dana kada ne znam šta da radim']. *Ima Dana* is also the name of a tavern in Skadarlija. See the next note.

p. 5, *Skadarlija*: pedestrian tree-lined cobbled street, full of taverns, that slopes down from a corner of Republic Square in the Centre of Belgrade to Bajlonova fruit and flower market off George Washington Street, in the direction of the Danube. If you go for a meal there in the evening, alone or in company, a costumed band will come to your table with violins and accordions, and sing you rich, sentimental songs ('Old Town Songs') often in haunting minor keys, and gypsy children may accost you, trying to sell you roses or carnations. The name *Skadarlija* is derived from 'Scandal', and at the turn of the 20th century it was a bohemian area, a mini-Montmartre or Plaka. But unlike those districts in Paris or Athens, it is still unspoilt by tourism, with its own unique and authentic Balkan flavour. See also the note to FISH SOUP, p. 150 below.

p. 5, *Mostar* [*most*: 'bridge'], capital of Hercegovina. The bridge was designed by the Ottoman architect Mimar Hayruddin during the reign of Sultan Suleiman the Magnificent, and completed in 1566. It took nine years to build, and as a result, the town became a thriving trading centre and crossroads between east and west. A single span stone arch bridge, 29 metres long and 20 metres above the water, it was an advanced technological feat for its time.

On November 9, 1993, during the war that broke up Yugoslavia, the bridge was destroyed by firing from a tank. It was rebuilt and reopened on July 23, 2004, by Charles, Prince of Wales.

The drawing of the bridge on the facing page was made in 1873 by the 22 year old Arthur Evans and included in his travel book, portentously entitled *Through Bosnia and the Herzegovina on Foot During the Insurrection, August and September, 1873, with an Historical Review of Bosnia and a Glimpse of the Croats, Slavonians and the Ancient Republic of Ragusa*. (Longmans, Green & Co, London, 1876, p. 344). The youthful Evans, later knighted for his excavations of Knossos, was wildly and pompously enthusiastic about the scenery – and equally wildly and pompously wrong about the history of the bridge, which he asserted to be of 'Roman origin'.

p. 5, *Novi Pazar*, town in the Sandžak region, southern Serbia, with a mixed Christian and Muslim population.

p. 6 'Nature and Society' and 'Artistic Culture' (i.e. 'Visual Arts'): subjects graded in school reports [respectively, 'Priroda i društvo' and 'likovna kultura'].

The Neretva Bridge, Mostar

p. 6, *Skopje*: capital of the Former Yugoslav Republic of Macedonia.

p. 6, *Baščaršija*: market district of Sarajevo.

p. 6, *Vodnik*: district of Belgrade.

p. 6, *Zoološki vrt* ['zoological garden']: Belgrade.

p. 6, *Palilula* and *Dedinje*, districts of Belgrade.

pp. 6–7, *Vojvode Stepe, Sremska, Nušićeva, Kneza Miloša*: streets in Belgrade.

p. 7, *Autokomanda*: road and motorway intersection, Belgrade.

p. 7, *Avala*: hill south of Belgrade, whose radio and TV tower took a direct hit from NATO bombs in 1999. They avoided bombing the monument there by Ivan Meštrović.

p. 7, *Šumadija, Banat, Vojvodina*: regions of Serbia.

p. 8, *Zeleni Venac, Bajlonova, Kalenić, Dušanova. Zemun, Djeram*: names of markets in and around Belgrade.

p. 8, *Mileševa, Dečani, Sopoćani, Morača, Studenica, Ćuprija*: Serbian monasteries.

p. 8–9, *Karaburma, Zvezdara, Slavija, Studentski Trg* ['Student Square']: places in Belgrade.

p. 9, *Knez Mihajlova* ['Duke Michael's']: pedestrian street in central Belgrade.

p. 9, *Kod Konja* ['At the Horse']: nickname of the bronze equestrian statue of Prince Michael, in Republic Square, Belgrade, and also the name of an open air café near the statue. The statue, by the Italian sculptor Enrico Pazzi, was put up in 1882 to celebrate the full liberation of Serbia from Turkish occupation.

p. 9, *Šabac*: town in central Serbia, and site of a Nazi concentration camp where in autumn 1941 many atrocities were committed, including mass murders. Victims were forced to run and were shot down while they vainly attempted to flee. *Klenak*: village eight kilometres from Šabac, to which prisoners were forced to run for the entire distance. *Sajmište*: Nazi concentration camp for women and children in Belgrade-Zemun, where the last victims from Šabac perished, as did others from all over Serbia. The full history of this and other camps, and how people were rounded up for them, remains to be told, including the role of Serbian quislings serving in Dimitrije Ljotić's collaborationist *Srpski dobrovoljački odred* ['Serbian Volunteer Detachment'].

p. 10, *Goli Otok* ['Naked Island'] and *Sveti Grgur* ['Saint Gregory']: two small Adriatic islands, in the strait between the larger island of Rab and the Dalmatian mainland. Following the break between Josip Broz Tito and Josef Stalin, between 1949 and 1956 these two islands served Tito as concentration camps for political prisoners. Conditions ranged from barbaric harshness to torture and atrocity. Internees included not only former revolutionaries, partisans and Communist party members known to be hard-line Stalinists, but a wide range of citizens with no oppositional political leanings, who were interned for often bizarre reasons and sometimes no reason at all. The men's camp was on *Goli Otok* and the women's on *Grgur*.

Suggestions have been made that the name *Goli Otok* originated not in the barrenness of the terrain but in a nudist camp on the island between the two world wars.

p. 10, *Postojnska jama*: a huge limestone cave system, 20 km long, 35 km from Trieste, in south-western Slovenia.

p. 10, 'brotherhood and unity': a reference to *'Bratstvo i jedinstvo'*, one of the best known Socialist slogans of Titoist Yugoslavia.

p. 10, *Poslednja šansa* ['The Last Chance']: restaurant in the centre of Tašmajdan Park, Belgrade.

p. 10, *Ohrid*: town on Lake Ohrid in the Republic of Macedonia. A species of pink fleshed trout is peculiar to its waters. *Ada Ciganlija*: island on the River Sava, Belgrade, known for its many restaurants on barges and boats moored to the banks.

p. 11, *Vračar*: part of Belgrade.

p. 11, *Jurija Gagarina*: avenue in New Belgrade, named after the Russian astronaut, Yuri Gagarin, the first man in space in 1961.

p. 11, 'struggle for a better life': reference to *Bolji život* ['A Better Life'], title of an ironic Belgrade-based TV soap opera around 1987–9. It mercilessly parodied all aspects of life in Socialist Yugoslavia and was regularly watched by viewers from all parts of the Federation.

p. 12, *Vranje*: town in south eastern Serbia, near the Bulgarian and Macedonian borders.

p. 12, *Požarevac*: provincial Serbian town, with the dubious distinction of being the birthplace of Slobodan Milošević. In 435 AD, under the name of *Margus*, it was the site for a treaty between Attila the Hun and the Byzantine Empire and, in 1718, for another pact called the

Treaty of Passarowitz, between Austria, Venice and the Ottoman Empire. This marked the end of the war of 1716–18 and, among other decisions, marked a limit on Ottoman northward expansion in the Balkans.

p. 12, *Pirot*, town in south-eastern Serbia, not far from the Bulgarian border: located half-way between Niš and Sofia.

p. 12, 'bound to get better' etc: an implicit reference to the common cheering and optimistic expression in Serbian and Croatian, 'biće bolje' ['things'll get better'].

p. 13, *Terazije*: street in central Belgrade.

p. 13, *Skupština*: Parliament.

p. 13, *Srebrenica*: town in Bosnia, site of the massacre in July 1995 of Muslim males, by units of the Army of the Serbian Republic [*VRS, Vojska Republike Srpske*] under the command of General Ratko Mladić. Gangs of volunteers (so-called 'paramilitary units') from Serbia took part with barbaric enthusiasm. It is estimated that over a period of five days, up to 8,000 men and boys, all Bosnian Muslims, were separated from their womenfolk by the Bosnian Serb troops. They were then executed in fields, schools and warehouses and buried in mass graves near Srebrenica. The town of Srebrenica had been declared the world's first 'United Nations safe haven', under the protection of a battalion of Dutch UN peacekeepers, but their members, who knew what was going on, stood helplessly by. The international community had pledged to protect the town, but failed miserably to do so. Only a few of the perpetrators have been brought to justice. Most notorious of the paramilitary units were the 'Scorpions', led by Slobodan Medić, a Serb from the town of Šid in Vojvodina. See 'Dejan Anastasijević, 'Trial of the Scorpions', http://www.ex-yupress.com/vreme/vreme 126.html; and 'Serb 'Scorpions' guilty of Srebrenica massacre', http:// www.guardian.co.uk/yugo/article/o,,2053972,00.html, accessed September 12, 2007.

p. 13, *Krajina*: ['Frontier'] or, more properly, *Vojna Krajina* ('Military Frontier'), from *kraj* ['edge, end'; compare the name *Ukraine*]: region in Croatia which, until 1995, was inhabited mainly by Serbs, who had been settled there since 1630, when they were given duties and rights as frontier-guards by the Hapsburg emperor along the border between the Austrian Empire and the Turkish Empire. See the note on *Vlachs*, p. 142 above. In the wake of the collapse of Yugoslavia, the forced expulsion (ethnic cleansing) of these Serbs in 1995 by the independent Croatian government headed by Franjo Tudžman was the outcome of an agreement made in London between Warren Christopher, the 63rd American Secretary of State, the German Foreign Minister Klaus Kinkel, and the Croatian diplomat Miomir Žužul. See Greg Elich, 'The Invasion of Serbian Krajina'', http://emperors-clothes.com/articles/elich/krajina.html; accessed October 2006 and September 2007.

p. 15, *Nebesna*: 'heavenly'.

BY THE BANKS OF THE SAVA, pp. 17–26

A series of memorial tablets dedicated to the men, women and children murdered by Croatian Fascists (*Ustaše*) at Jasenovac and Stara

Gradiška concentration camps and other locations during the Second World War.

Following the Nazi invasion and dismemberment of Yugoslavia in April 1941, the 'Independent State of Croatia' was established as a pro-Nazi government. Its ideology was concocted from a mixture of Nazism, Italian Fascism and an extremist local form of Roman Catholic fanaticism. The Ustaša dictatorship inaugurated its racial policies as soon as it came into power. Between August 1941 and April 1945, the systematic annihilation of all Serbs, Jews and Romas living within the Croatian borders, as well as of anti-Fascists of many nationalities, took place at the death camp known as Jasenovac, a complex of five major and three smaller 'special' camps, spread out over 240 sq. km. in south-central Croatia. The word jasen means 'ash tree'.

Estimates of the total numbers of men, women and children killed at Jasenovac range from 70,000 to 700,000 and it will never be possible to establish accurate figures. The regime so far exceeded the Nazi camps in its barbarism and savagery that even German officials claimed to be shocked. Whereas an almost predictable, factory-like organised monotony prevailed in the camps run by Germans, the Jasenovac authorities specialised in vengeful unpredictability and 'artistic' variation and inventiveness in the sadistic application of torture and murder. General von Horstenau, Hitler's representative in Zagreb, wrote in his personal diary for 1942 that the Ustaša camps in Croatia were 'the epitome of horror' and Arthur Hefner, a German transport officer for work forces in the Reich, wrote on November 11, 1942: 'The concept of the Jasenovac camp should actually be understood as several camps which are several kilometres apart, grouped around Jasenovac. Regardless of the propaganda, this is one of the most horrible of camps, which can only be compared to Dante's Inferno.' See http://www.jasenovac.org/whatwasjasenovac.php, the website of the Jasenovac Research Institute, accessed, August 2007.

The full scale of the crimes committed at Jasenovac has never been fully admitted by successive government authorities, let alone systematically investigated, either during the post-war Tito era (1945–1980) or during the post-Tito period when Croatia was still part of Yugoslavia (1980–1991). After the break-up of the Federation, obfuscation continued under the presidency of Croatian president Franjo Tudjman (1991–2000), who was notorious for his statements of Holocaust denial and revisionism. Thus, deliberate and systematic attempts to shroud or whitewash truth, destroy evidence and make the site unreadable have been made by successive authorities and regimes. However, since 2000, thanks in large part to current pressure on Croatia from the European Union, under the current presidency of Stipe Mesić, a former Communist and the final president of the Socialist Federation of Yugoslavia, some progress has been made in the direction of admitting that the crimes did take place.

The source for the photographs that accompany the text is The Crimes of the Fascist Occupants and their Collaborators Against Jews in Yugoslavia (Federation of Jewish Communities of the Federative People's Republic of Yugoslavia, Belgrade, 1957), otherwise known as the

'Black Book', pp. 225–245.

The sequence is retrospectively dedicated to Cadik I. Danon Braco, author of the extraordinary testament *The Smell of Human Flesh: A Witness of the Holocaust, Memories of Jasenovac* (tr. Vidosava Janković, Dosije, Belgrade, 2000). Born in 1918 into a Sephardic family in Sarajevo, Braco Danon was imprisoned in Jasenovac at the age of 18. He survived nine months there. On September 12, 1942, he managed to escape with six other inmates. He joined the Partisans and fought with them till the end of the war. He then had a distinguished career as an architect. I was privileged to meet him at the Writers' Association in Belgrade, May 2007 and again in Belgrade, in October 2007.

p. 17. The epigraph quotes the last sentences in Braco Danon's book, pp. 178–9, in my slightly modified translation.

p. 23, 'bring parsley, fennel, rosemary, rue.' See Ophelia's speeches: 'There's rosemary, that's for remembrance' and ' There's fennel for you, and columbines; there's rue for you, and here's some for me; we may call it herb of grace o' Sundays. O! you must wear your rue with a difference.' William Shakespeare, *Hamlet*, V. 2. 174 and 176–183.

p. 25. The photograph of Engineer Rosenberg was taken in the concentration camp of Lepoglava, near Varaždin in northern Croatia.

'Bring poppies, agapanthi, asphodel'. The Greeks associated poppies with sleep and asphodel with death. For agapanthi (etym. 'love flowers'), see George Seferis's poem, 'Stratis Thalassinos among the Agapanthi', *Collected Poems*, tr. Edmund Keeley and Philip Sherrard, Jonathan Cape, London, 1969, pp. 279–282.

This sequence was written in Cambridge, December 27 and 28, 2005, following conversations about Jasenovac with David Llewellyn Burdett.

MI DVA, p. 29

I am indebted to Ana Jelnikar for explaining *mi dva* to me. 'Deathful He' refers to Lawrence Ferlinghetti's poem 'He': 'And he is the mad eye of the fourth person singular / of which nobody speaks / and he is the voice of the fourth person singular / in which nobody speaks / and which yet exists / with a long head and a foolscap face / and the long mad hair of death / of which nobody speaks.' *The New American Poetry 1945–1960*, ed. Donald M. Allen, Grove Press, New York, 1960, p. 136. See also POEM ON THE SPRING EQUINOX, p. 50.

SEAGULL'S WINGS, p. 30

Drafted, Cambridge, August 4, 2004; revised, July 12, 2007; completed August 3–4, 2007.

NOTES FROM THREE CITIES, pp. 31–33

Written in Belgrade and Zemun, 1987–89.

1. A WALLET, p. 31

'Vašintonova': Washington Street.

2. WHITE CHERRIES, p. 32
Dedicated to Jasna B. Mišić. In Serbian, white and black cherries have different names: respectively, *trešnje* and *višnje*.

3. FISH SOUP, p. 33
'Smederevo': see the note, p. 141 above, and the next poem.

Ima dana kada ne znam šta da radim: 'There are days when I don't know what to do': the first line of a haunting love song in the genre of 'Old Town Songs'. *Ima dana* is a famous tavern, named after the song, in *Skadarlija*. See also the note on p. 144 above.

ON THE QUALITIES OF LIGHT IN THE BALKANS, pp. 34–35
The setting is the medieval fort at Smederevo, overlooking the Danube. Some of the poem embeds impressions of a walk along the castle battlements with Ivan V. Lalić, his translator Francis Jones, and Hanifa da Lipi, on October 27 1983, before I gave a poetry reading that evening, introduced by Ivan Lalić, at the 'Smederevo Autumn' poetry festival ('Smederevska pesnička jesen'). Lalić himself wrote several poems relating to this location, notably 'Smederevo' and 'The Danube by Smederevo'. See *The Works of Love*, tr. Francis R. Jones, Anvil Press Poetry, London, 1981, pp. 16 & 19. Written in Cambridge, 8–13 August 1999.
'separated trays / of candles lit for the living and the dead'. In Orthodox churches, two trays are provided. See also p. 14, 'sand-trays / for spindly yellow candles perched on wooden tripods'.
'white angel, with darkening, blue tipped wings': Mileševa Monastery, see also the front cover, and the poems on pp. 52–55 and 92.
'the certain chime of light / from eye to eye, as glass rings against glass'. See 'A Grove of Trees and a Grove of Stones':

> In Yugoslavia, ordinary people still look each other directly in the eyes when they talk to each other. This frank, clear look occurs ritually, for example, whenever two people toast one another, raising their glasses not just with a wish for 'Good Health', as in my country, but for life itself ('Živeli!'). Foreigners do not always notice this, but when they do, this simple, courteous acknowledgement of the full humanity of other people is seen as a radiant grace, a great treasure, a complete recognition of connectedness. (http://www.richardburns.eu/site/Grove-of-trees.html, accessed July 23, 2008.)

POEM AT THE AUTUMN EQUINOX, pp. 36–37
Written in Cambridge, September 1999. Dedicated to Arijana Mišić-Burns.

FRAGMENT: ON *THE SEPHARAD*, pp. 38–39

Sepharad is a place-name of uncertain location, whose only biblical mention is in the Book of Obadiah. After the 2nd century A.D., the location was identified with the Iberian peninsula: hence, the word 'Sephardic' describing Jews originating from this region; and hence also the Modern Hebrew words *Sfarad* 'Spain', *Sfaradi* (m) and *Sfaradiya* (f) 'Spaniard', *Sfaradim* 'Spaniards' and *Sfaradit* 'Spanish language'. After the expulsion of Jews from Spain in 1492, many Sephardic Jews emigrated to the Balkans and established communities, especially in Salonika, Skopje and Sarajevo. They spoke Ladino, a Romance language derived mainly from Old Castilian, with smatterings of Hebrew, Greek, Turkish and South Slavonic languages stirred into it.

The text is dedicated to the memory of Eugen Verber (1923–1996), polymath, professor of Talmudic Studies at Sarajevo, prolific writer, translator, character actor, bon viveur and editor of the *Sarajevo Haggadah* (1983). When I presented this version to him in typescript, he spent several hours searching for references to its author, Salamon Ruben ben Israel of Salonika. For clues to the identity of this personage, see the fourth and last lines of the next poem, IN WAR: JUNE 4, 1943, pp. oo and oo above. For biographical information on Verber, see Predrag Palavestra, *Jewish Writers in Serbian Literature*, tr. George Nikolić, ASWA, London, 2003, pp. 131–2.

The text was written in Belgrade, 1990, triggered by working on a translation of the first chapters of *Miris kiše na Balkanu* ['*Scent of Rain in the Balkans*'], Gordana (Krstić) Kuić's first novel, which is set in Sarajevo.

A Serbo-Croat translation by Jasna Levinger-Goy of this text was published with the English version in *SaLon* No. 9, bulletin of the Jewish Association 'Prijatelji La Benevolencija', London, 1998.

IN WAR: JUNE 4, 1943, pp. 40–43

A 'found poem', written in Cambridge, 1985–6. Italicised lines are quoted, with small changes, from F. W. Deakin, *The Embattled Mountain*, Oxford University Press, 1971, pp. 48–49. Deakin was an Oxford historian and British officer. On Churchill's orders he was parachuted from Derna in North Africa into the central command of the Yugoslav partisans on the night of May 27–28, 1943. He arrived perilously, in the middle of savage fighting between Germans and partisans on Mount Durmitor. Deakin's reports to Churchill, as well as those of his better known successor Fitzroy MacLean, were instrumental factors in swinging British support towards Josip Broz Tito and his Communist partisans in 1943, and away from Draža Mihajlović, the Royalist (*četnik*) commander and Minister of Defence for the exiled Yugoslav Government.

When I wrote this piece, I had not yet been able to read *The Rape of Serbia: The British Role in Tito's Grab for Power 1943–1944* (Harcourt Brace Jovanovich, San Diego, 1990) by Michael Lees, a British officer billeted with Mihajlović's forces in Serbia. Published after the release of secret British documents about World War 2 under the 50 year provision,

Lees' book challenged the official Yugoslav and British post-war version of the Communists' 'monopoly' on heroism. His book paints a vivid picture of the struggle of Mihajlović's units and their abandonment by the Allies.

The rest of the poem is a collage of information from miscellaneous British newspapers, May 30–June 6, 1943.

p. 42, '*Sandžak*': a region lying along the border between Serbia and Montenegro, around Novi Pazar. The name originates in the Turkish word for 'standard or 'banner' ('sancak'), which denoted an administrative district in the Ottoman Empire.

TABLET FOR LILI BÖHM, p. 44

Lili Böhm was a member of a Serbian Jewish youth organisation. She was hanged with other young Serbs and Jews by Nazi occupiers in the courtyard of a military barracks in Novi Sad in Autumn 1941. Source for photograph: *The Crimes of the Fascist Occupants and their Collaborators Against Jews in Yugoslavia* (Belgrade, 1957), p. 242. See also the next note and BY THE BANKS OF THE SAVA, pp. 17–26, and the note on that sequence of poems, on p. 148 above. Written in Cambridge, 28 December 2005.

TABLET FOR A SLAVE LABOURER, p. 45

Source: *ibid*, p. 245. The photograph is of the exhumed corpse of an unknown Jewish slave-labourer, forced by the Nazis to work in the Bor mines, Eastern Serbia. It was taken in Crvenka, a town in Vojvodina, northern Serbia.

This poem is also an indirect tribute to the Hungarian Jewish poet, Miklós Radnóti, who was a slave-labourer in the same mines. As the Nazis evacuated the Balkans in 1944, like the unknown victim in the photograph, Radnóti was one of a group of prisoners who were force-marched back up through Serbia. In November 1944, he was shot by Hungarian fascist troops and buried in a mass grave near Abda in Hungary. For English versions of Radnóti's last poems, found in his raincoat pocket when his body was exhumed, plus more information, see Miklós Radnóti, *Forced March*, tr. Clive Wilmer and George Gomori (Carcanet, 1980), and *Camp Notebook*, tr. Francis Jones (Arc, 2000). This poem was written in Cambridge, 28 December 2005.

POEM AT THE SPRING EQUINOX, pp. 46–51

Written in Cambridge, 16–17 March 1999, and July–August 2007. Section 4, p. 50, 'the mad eye of the fourth person singular': see the note on MI DVA, p. 149 above.

POEM FOR MY INFANT DAUGHTER AT MILEŠEVA MONASTERY, pp. 52–55

For the fresco of the *White Angel* ['*Beli andjeo*'], see the front cover of this book. See also Peter Russell's poem, 'To the Holy Virgin of Mileševa', written in Venice, 1969, in his *All for the Wolves, Selected Poems 1947–1975*, Anvil Press Poetry, London, 1984. Written in Belgrade, August 1989. Copied and revised slightly, in Ballyhealy, County Wexford, August 22, 1999. Dedicated to Arijana Mišić-Burns, as are the next two poems.

    p. 53, 'blue angel'. I have let this error stand. It was not triggered only by the Marlene Deitrich film. Thinking of my sequence of poems *The Blue Butterfly*, I must have subliminally confuted the word *beli* with an image of blueness. In fact this angel's wings *are* black fringed with blue. The Serbian for 'blue' is *plavi*. To confuse matters more, the Greek word for 'sky blue' is *galanos*, from *gala* ('milk'): another ambivalence between blueness and whiteness. I wonder if the image of 'milky' embedded here is at least partly explained by 'The Milky Way' being a metonym for the entire heaven – though the sky is not exactly 'blue' at night time. Blue milk?

    p. 53, *božidar*: 'gift of God'.

    p. 54, 'the wisdom of these sages': that is, of the saints portrayed in the frescoes. See W. B. Yeats' line in 'Sailing to Byzantium': 'Oh sages standing in God's holy fire'.

POEM FOR A VERY SMALL CHILD, pp. 56
Written in Cambridge, 25 October 2002.

FATHER TO SMALL CHILD, p. 57
Written on Tenerife, Summer 1993.

BORDERERS, pp. 58–63
Dedicated to Philip Kuhn.

BORDERERS, RESIDENT GHOSTS and AUDITORS, pp. 53–60, drafted in Cambridge, August 9, 2004; completed July 12 and August 3, 2007.

LONGING, p. 61, drafted in Berlin and Cambridge, August 19 and September 11, 2002; completed July 11–13 and August 4, 2007.

ELSEWHERES, p. 62, drafted in Cambridge, August 9, 2004; completed July 12 and August 3, 2007.

NOW I CONFESS, p. 63, drafted, Cambridge, February 24, 2000; completed July 12, 2007.

BY THE DANUBE, ZEMUN, pp. 64
Composed on 10 January 1990, in the wake of the Romanian revolution (17–25 December 1989) that overthrew the dictatorship of Nicolae Ceauşescu. Georgi Georgiju Deža Street in Zemun was named after Gheorghe Gheorghiu-Dej, Romanian communist leader, 1948–1965. Since the collapse of Yugoslavia, the street has been renamed *Aleksinačkih rudara* ('Aleksinac Miners').

    Dedicated to Jasna B. Mišić.

TO ZORA, p. 65
Zora: 'Dawn', and a woman's name. Written in Cambridge, December 1997.

GUESTS, p. 66
Written in Cambridge, 1999.

EPIGRAPH, p. 67
Ivan V. Lalić, 'The Voice Singing in the Garden', tr. Francis Jones, *The Works of Love*, Anvil Press Poetry, London, 1981, p. 14; George Seferis, 'Stratis Thalassinos among the Agapanthi', tr. Edmund Keeley and Philip Sherrard, *Collected Poems 1924–1955*, Jonathan Cape, London, 1969, p. 279.

WHOSE VOICE? and WHO CAN I ASK, pp. 69 and 70
Written in Belgrade, 1988.

THE VOICE IN THE GARDEN, pp. 71–74
Written in Belgrade, 1988. Several textual changes have been made in the second and third stanzas from the version that appeared in the first edition of this book (2004). Serbian translation published in *Polje* (Novi Sad, November 1989), tr. Bogdana B. Bobić.

IN THE MIRROR, p. 75
Written, Cambridge, August 8, 1999.

HILL OF THE FOUNTAINS, p. 76
Written in Cambridge and Ballyhealy between July 20 and September 25, 1999.

THE STORK, p. 77
Drafted, Cambridge, July 3, 2004; revised, January 3, 2007; finalised, August 9, 2007. Based on an experience in 1967, when I worked as a language teacher in the Albanian-speaking village of Kriekouki (Plataea), Greece. I was standing on the single-storey roof of the schoolroom, when I watched the flight of a stork.

THE GARMENT OF DEATH, p. 78
Recalling and commemorating the philosopher Gillian Rose (September 28, 1947–December 10, 1995). Images in the third stanza derive from legends of the descent of Astarte/Ishtar into the underworld. Written in Ballyhealy, Summer 1988.

POEM FOR ANDJELKA, p. 79
Written in Cambridge, Autumn 1998, for Andjelka Samardžić-Soškić: born 20 November 20, 1950; died of cancer, December 21, 1998.

NED GOY HAS GONE OUT, pp. 80–81
Edward Dennis Goy (September 22, 1926–March 13, 2000) was a fellow of Queens' College, Cambridge. He taught Serbo-Croatian literature and language at the Faculty of Modern Languages at Cambridge University. Coinciding with the imminent break-up of Yugoslavia, his retirement from lecturing in 1990 was the signal for Cambridge to remove Serbo-Croat from its syllabus. He was the leading expert on

Croatian and Serbian literature in Britain and one of the foremost authorities on South Slav culture and history throughout Europe. My obituary for him appeared in *The Times*, London, March 23, 2000. The poem was written on a train from Figline (Tuscany) to Rome, in June 2000, and completed in Cambridge in the days immediately following my return.

To write simply again, p. 82

First draft, January 23, 2000; revised and completed, January 25, 2000. Retrospectively dedicated to the memory of Haša Popa, whose ashes were placed on the grave of her husband, the poet Vasko Popa (1922–1991), in the New Cemetery, Belgrade, on Thursday, October 18, 2001. Melanie Rein and I attended this ceremony with at the invitation of the Belgrade writer, Moma Dimić. 'Brass over graves': in Serbia, as in some other eastern and south eastern European countries, gypsy brass bands play at funerals.

Tonight the war ended, p. 83

Written in Cambridge, June 1999. A Serbian translation by Jasna B. Mišić was published in *Knjizevene novine*, Belgrade, October 15, 1999.

I dreamed I slept, p. 84

Triggered by a note by Ivo Andrić, 'I dreamed that I was sleeping', in his *Conversation with Goya, Bridges, Signs*, tr. Celia Hawkesworth, Menard Press & the School of Slavonic and East European Studies, London, 1992, p. 73. Written in Cambridge, December 1 & 2, 2002. Dedicated retrospectively to the memory of Felicia Burns, née Jacob (born, Gura Humora, Romania, July 31, 1948; died, Jerusalem, September 27, 2004). Felicia married my cousin, Ronnie Burns, on September 13, 1970.

Bogomil, p. 85

The title: etym. *Bog* 'God', *milost* 'kindness, gentleness, sweetness'. The Bogomils were members of a Manichean sect that originated in 10th century Bulgaria and spread westwards into Serbia, Bosnia and Hercegovina. Their dualistic beliefs contained underlying elements of Gnosticism, Zoroastrianism and Mithraism. Members of the sect were thoroughly persecuted: by Rome, Byzantium and Bulgarian and Serbian dynasties. One theory is that when the Turks overran the Balkan Christian States in the fifteenth century, the Bogomils of Bosnia rapidly converted to Islam. If it were not for the unfortunate fact that few if any remnants of Bogomilism have survived in Bosnia, the history of the Bogomils might provide a helpful key to understanding some contemporary political and religious conflicts. Bogomilism is shrouded in considerable mystery. Written in Cambridge, March 17–23, 2002. Dedicated to Francis R. Jones.

Night, Summer, p. 86

Written in Cambridge, June 1998. Dedicated to Melanie Rein.

MEMORY, SUMMER, pp. 87–89

Written in Cambridge, August 19, 2006, after reading *Poems* (ASA, London 2003) by Jovan (Vava) Hristić (1933–2002), translated by Bernard Johnstone (1933–2003). Both these men were my friends and this poem is dedicated to their memories. The poem was finalised in July and August 2007.

SILKEN THREAD : GYPSY'S SONG and SILKEN THREAD : POET'S PAGES, pp. 90–91

Svilen konac ['Silken Thread']: title of a haunting melody and also the name of a well-known Belgrade instrumental group. Written in Cambridge, September 1999.

THE FACE OF LIGHT, p. 92

Written in Ballyhealy and Cambridge, August-September, 1999. In line 9, for the 'white angel, with darkening, blue tipped wings', see the front cover and the poems on pp. 34–35 and 52–53. A Serbian translation by Jasna B. Mišić was published in *Knjizevene novine*, Belgrade, October 15, 1999.

THE VOICE OF LIGHT, p. 93

My father, Alexander Burns (Berengarten) died on his 46th birthday, May 10, 1947. *Zemun, Ušče, Kalemegdan*: for these place names, see the notes on pp. 143 and 145 above. Written in Zemun, June 1989, and revised in Ballyhealy and Cambridge, August–September, 1999.

HARVEST, p. 94

Written in Warwick, October 25, 1998; developed and revised in Cambridge, November 1998 and December 2001; completed July 19, 2007.

THE MAN I MET ON THE HILL, p. 95

Written in Cambridge, August 12, 1985. Dedicated to the memory of Octavio Paz (March 31, 1914–April 19, 1998). I was lucky enough to know him when I was a young man in 1971–2, when he spent a year in Cambridge. My 'Avebury' was also dedicated to him: see *For the Living*, Salt, 2008, pp. 23–50.

ON THE DEATH OF IVAN V. LALIĆ, pp. 97–118

Ivan V. Lalić was born in Belgrade on June 8, 1931 and died in Belgrade on 27 July 27, 1996. My obituary for him appeared in *The Times*, London, August 5, 1996. The poems were written in Cambridge between 1996 and 2007. Epigraphs, p. 97: Ivan V. Lalić, 'Song for the Dead', *A Rusty Needle*, tr. Francis R. Jones, Anvil Press Poetry, London, 1996, p. 42; and James Burns Singer, *The Collected Poems of Burns Singer*, ed. W. A. S. Keir, Secker & Warburg, London, 1970, p. 73.

THIS DOOR I CAN'T UNLATCH, p. 99

First version, Cambridge, 1999–2000, revised, July 12, 2007; finalised, August 9, 2007.

WHAT DID YOU MEAN BY IT? p. 100

'the night of harvest princesses': August 15. The reference is to a Balkan village custom at harvest-time involving young girls dressed in white. They are called *Kraljice*, 'princesses'. First version, Cambridge, December 17, 1999; revised, Feburary 24, 2000 and November 15, 2001; finalised, August 27, 2007.

ONE DAY YOU WAKE UP, pp. 101–102

First version, Cambridge, May 15, 1999; revised, Ballyhealy, August 19 & 20, 1999, and Cambridge, 27th December 27, 1999 & January 15, 2000; finalised, Cambridge, April 11, 2000.

ARE YOU THERE? pp. 103–104

Drafted, Cambridge, December 25–27, 1999; revised January 2, 2000; finalised, January 15, 2000.

EVEN WHEN YOU LIVED, p. 105

'Rovinj seabed': Ivan Lalić and his wife Branča spent their summers in Rovinj, on the Croatian coast. I am indebted to Branka Lalic for this information.

'Black snows of darkness /melted by a candle flame': see Ivan V. Lalić's poem 'Wick': 'Darkness is but a handful of blackish snow / melting on the fire of my miracle's glow.' *A Rusty Needle*, tr. Francis R. Jones, 1996, p. 43.

'Thracian, Dacian, Phrygian, Illyrian': ancient and extinct Balkan languages, with few extant inscriptions.

'Etruscan': extinct non-Indo-European language of Italy; with many extant inscriptions. The Etruscans gave their name to modern Tuscany.

Phersipnai Prsepna Phersipnei. Etruscan names for the Queen of the Underworld, derived from Greek *Persephone*. Compare Latin *Proserpina*.

'Rhodope': mountain range, birthplace of Orpheus, in Thrace, a region mostly now belonging to southern Bulgaria and a small part to northern Greece.

Written in Cambridge between July 17 and August 30, 2007.

NOBODY DIES TOO LATE, p. 106

The title is taken from Ivan V. Lalić's poem 'Song for the Dead', *A Rusty Needle*, tr. Francis R. Jones, 1996, p. 42, as is the phrase 'lords of the far side': See also the epigraph on p. 97 above. First drafted, Cambridge, August 1999; revised and finalised, July 15–August 9, 2007.

LORDS OF THE FAR SIDE, p. 107

For the title, see the previous note. First drafted, Cambridge, August 1999; revised and finalised, July 14–August 15, 2007.

THE UNREADY ONES, p. 108

First drafted in Cambridge, August 10–11, 1999; revised and completed, July 7–August 9, 2007.

NOT THE DEAD BUT DEATH, p. 109
Written in Cambridge, July 7–July 30, 2007.

NOTHING, HOLLOW RING, p. 110
Cambridge, July 14–August 9, 2007.

ONE IOTA OF RESPECT? p. 111
Line 12, 'for the living' reiterates the title of Volume I in my *Selected Writings* and the dedication to *The Blue Butterfly*. Written in Cambridge, July 11–September 1, 2007.

TISSUE OF WATERFALLS, p. 112
Drafted in Cambridge, August 10–11, 1999; revised and finalised, July 11–August 30, 2007.

FROM THE OTHER SHORE, p. 113–114
Drafted in Ballyhealy and Cambridge, August 1999; revised and finalised, Cambridge, July 17–August 9, 2007.

ARISTOCRATS OF SILENCE, p. 115
'Kosmaj': hill near Mladenovac in Serbia, not far from Belgrade, a holiday area well known for its natural beauty. Ivan Lalić spent summers there as a boy. I am indebted to Branka Lalić for this information. Written in Cambridge, July 15–August 8, 2007.

DICTATED BY A MAN WHO IS DEAD, p. 116
Drafted in Cambridge, late 1998; revised, August 5–11, 1999; finalised August 9–September 1, 2007.

BACKGROUNDED AMONG THESE, p. 117
Drafted, Cambridge, July 11–14, 2007; revised July 11–14 & August 8–10, 2007; finalised August 30, 2007.

THE BOWL OF LIGHT FILLS AND EMPTIES, p. 118
Written, Cambridge, July 7–17, 2007.

THINGS IN THEIR MIRACLES, pp. 119–125
Epigraphs, p. 119: Lynne McTaggart, *The Field*, Element Books, London, 2003, p. 160; and Slobodan Rakitić, 'Pesnik u vlasti leptira' ['Poet in the power of a butterfly'], in Richard Burns, *Plavi leptir* ['The Blue Butterfly'], tr. Vera V. Radojević, Plava Tačka, Zemun, 2007 (p. 153). See also his source in Jean Chevalier and Alain Geerbrandt, *Dictionary of Symbols*, (Penguin Books, London, p. 378). The sequence draws on preliminary versions made in Cambridge, January 8, 2000, after waking at 4.30 a.m. and writing notes down 'straight out of dream'. My journal entry records: 'In the dream I was collating different drafts of "The Flight of the Imago" when a line with very clear words demanded to be added. But the moment I put pen to paper it had gone. I persisted, though, and this is what came out.' This version, based on these notes, was written in Cambridge, August 24–27, 2007,

after reading Slobodan Rakitić's essay on *The Blue Butterfly*. The sequence is dedicated to Slobodan Rakitić and also to the memory of Valerie, wife of my cousin, Michael Grosvenor-Myer (April 13, 1935–August 9, 2007). My obituary for her appeared in *The Times*, August 16, 2007.

PURE BLUE, AND COOL, p. 121
The last line refers to a sentence in Slobodan Rakitić's essay quoted in the previous note: 'Of all colours, blue is the deepest and most 'transparent': it symbolises a non-material, metaphysical (meta-real) world. Blue is considered to be the 'coolest' and, in its absolute value, purest of all colours.' op. cit, p. 115, tr. Vera V. Radojević. See also the note on POEM FOR MY INFANT DAUGHTER AT MILEŠEVA MONASTERY, pp. 152–153 above.

FINGER OF LIFE, FINGER OF THE WORLD, p. 122
For the source in Slobodan Rakitić, see EPIGRAPH, p. 119 and the note above.

RECALLING ŠUMARICE, pp. 129–130
The poem revisits the themes and inception of *The Blue Butterfly* (Salt Publishing, Cambridge, 2008). Written in Cambridge, August 2007.

WHEN DEATH'S DOOR WAS LOCKED, pp. 131
Written in Cambridge, February 24–25, 2000; revised April 5, 2000.

TOPČIDER, OCTOBER, p. 132
Topčider: large wooded park on the outskirts of Belgrade. First drafted in Warwick, October 25, 1998; revised in Cambridge, November 24, 1998; and finalised in Cambridge between August 9 and 26, 2007.

THE APPLE, p. 133
Written in Cambridge, May 27–28, 2007, shortly after meeting historian Staniša Brkić and poet Slobodan Pavičević in Kragujevac. The poem is dedicated to them.

WOMAN READING, p. 134
Written in Cambridge, 1998. Dedicated to Melanie Rein.

FAITH, p. 135
Dedicated to Vera V. Radojević. Written in Cambridge, May 27–28, 2007, following meetings with her in Belgrade and Kragujevac.

RB
CAMBRIDGE
AUGUST 2, 2008